Praise for

"A revered scholar and beloved educator, john a. powell inspires us to believe in a world of belonging—and shows us how to labor for it. Wise and visionary, powell helps us find the courage to forge connections with others, the earth, and ourselves in order to transform the world from the inside out. *The Power of Bridging* is your essential guide for building a world of belonging, right where you are."

Valarie Kaur
bestselling author of *See No Stranger* and *Sage Warrior*

"john a. powell's vision for a world where we all belong is powerful and compelling, in large part because it's rooted in decades of values-based work advocating for civil and human rights. His ideas have inspired shifts in policy that have transformed people's daily lives, and his approach to justice questions has influenced countless activists and policymakers alike."

Michelle Alexander
New York Times bestselling author of *The New Jim Crow*

"With careful attention to the realities of fragmentation and the stories that reproduce it, john a. powell points us toward a better story—what he calls a 'bridging story'—that can help us find a bigger 'we.' This is the kind of work we need to build toward a Third Reconstruction of America."

Rev. Dr. William J. Barber II
author of *White Poverty* and *The Third Reconstruction*

"*The Power of Bridging* gives us the understanding and tools we need to recover the innate bonds we as human beings have with each other and invites us to actively build bridges across the generational, cultural, political, and ideological divides that shape our world. Both timely and timeless, this is a unique guide to help us navigate the challenges we face as a society."

Ai-jen Poo

cofounder and president of the National Domestic Workers Alliance, cofounder and director of Caring Across Generations, author of *The Age of Dignity*

"At a moment of great division and turmoil, john a. powell leads us toward each other, asking us to imagine a world many of us cannot: one where we all feel a deep sense of belonging and connection. This brilliant book is a must-read for all practitioners of social change, and for everyone committed to preserving and expanding multiracial democracy."

Deepak Bhargava

president of The JPB Foundation, coauthor of *Practical Radicals*

"We need john a. powell's call to bridging and belonging now more than ever. At a time when it seems as if our social fabric is broken and coming undone, powell lays out an intimate vision that is as inspiring as it is practical. Through an engaging narrative, this book empowers us all to become bridgers so we can all belong."

Rabbi Jonah Pesner

director of the Religious Action Center of Reform Judaism

"An insightful and moving exploration of belonging, bridging, and interconnectedness, this book challenges readers to embrace empathy and understanding in a world where everyone deserves to feel valued and accepted. A thought-provoking read by one of the most inspirational thinkers of our time who inspires us to have courageous conversations and encourages the critical shift towards a more inclusive and compassionate society."

Kumi Naidoo

former secretary general of Amnesty International
and executive director of Greenpeace

"*The Power of Bridging* is a page turner I would recommend to everyone. I was stunned how similar john's background was to my own, and though we took different paths in life, we somehow wound up in the same place in many ways. For sure, there is a wide gulf between my world, john's, and many others—which is why bridging is so necessary. All people are all places, and this book teaches us new skills of engagement that anyone can apply in their daily lives."

Pastor Bob Roberts Jr.

founder of GlocalNet, cofounder of the Multi-Faith Neighbors Network

"In *The Power of Bridging*, john a. powell shows us how to expand the tables we occupy by building bridges with those society has othered. By doing this, we can save the world we have and leave a better one for future generations. powell has personally changed my own life and approach to being human. His invitation to bridge, and innovation around social change, is a game changer that will be studied beyond our time."

Ben McBride

cofounder of Empower Initiative, author of *Troubling the Water*

The
Power of
Bridging

Also by john a. powell

*Racing to Justice: Transforming Our Conceptions of
Self and Other to Build an Inclusive Society*

*Belonging without Othering: How We Save Ourselves
and the World* (with Stephen Menendian)

The Power of Bridging

how to build a world
where we all belong

john a. powell

with Rachelle Galloway-Popotas

sounds true
BOULDER, COLORADO

Sounds True
Boulder, CO

Published 2024

Cover design by Jennifer Miles
Jacket design by Rachael Murray
Book design by Ranee Kahler

Printed in the United States of America

BK06761

Library of Congress Cataloging-in-Publication Data

Names: powell, john a., 1947- author. | Galloway-Popotas, Rachelle, author.
Title: The power of bridging : how to build a world where we all belong / by
    john a. powell, with Rachelle Galloway-Popotas.
Description: Boulder, CO : Sounds True Inc., 2024. | Includes bibliographical
    references and index.
Identifiers: LCCN 2024012230 (print) | LCCN 2024012231 (ebook) | ISBN
    9781649631657 (trade paperback) | ISBN 9781649631664 (ebook)
Subjects: LCSH: Toleration. | Discrimination. | Belonging (Social
    psychology)
Classification: LCC HM1271 .P69 2024 (print) | LCC HM1271
    (ebook) | DDC 179/.9--dc23/eng/20240430
LC record available at https://lccn.loc.gov/2024012230
LC ebook record available at https://lccn.loc.gov/2024012231

FSC
www.fsc.org
MIX
Paper | Supporting
responsible forestry
FSC® C103056

For Simone Grace powell
Alma Lamson powell
and all the children exposed to surplus suffering

Contents

Preface

It's impossible for me to talk about bridging without telling you the story of my father and mother.

In many ways, when I tell stories about my mother and father, about my childhood, and about my family, people hear tales of difficulty and struggle. Yet my father and mother had a fairy tale relationship. While struggle and difficulty were part of their lives, it was not their whole story.

Theirs was not a special story for me. It was my life, much of my world, and my foundation. It was only when I moved away and into a different world that I was able to reflect on the world I had come from, much as when we travel and live in different places, it helps bring the world we come from into a different focus.

So let me share with you some aspects of the story of my family as I have come to know it after I became an adult.

My parents, Marshall Powell Jr. and Florcie Mae Rimpson, met when they were just kids. My mother was fourteen, and my dad was sixteen. Of course, for much of Black America in the American South in the 1930s, and certainly for my parents, life had already thrust them into adulthood. They married two years after meeting and went on to have nine children, of which I'm the sixth.

As sharecroppers living in a segregated society, their lives were often challenging. Discrimination was an everyday reality for them, a social norm that was both accepted and disturbing. There was a degree of normalcy along with a concern for safety. The demands and joys of life would consume much of their available energy.

If I were to go into more detail about their difficulties, you might conclude, "What a hard, tough life. It sounds full of pain and sadness."

But if I could have you *meet* my parents and get to know them, I think you would experience just the opposite. You might instead say, "Wait, this life of scarcity that you just described, and these beautiful people standing here being graced with more joy than anyone could ask for—those two things don't quite fit. These people I'm meeting emanate a boundless and radiant love. They appear blessed."

And you would be right. They were blessed, as am I.

When I think of my parents, they were a beacon of love, with a light that drew people to them. Our house was always busy, not just full with nine kids but always also with other people coming over, just to be around my parents. Love was their language and their practice. People wanted to be in this space of love, and they would often claim our family as their own.

My mother was the matriarch of the family. Behind an easy smile, she had a quiet tenacity that presented a challenge to what was effectively in the larger world a racialized, and in our family a male, caste system. While my dad was the formally named head of the family, we all knew it was my mom who was really in charge. Her sense of justice and kindness was unshakeable. And she did not suffer fools. Well, except for my dad. The public and private face of my family were often quite different.

My father had the stature of a bodybuilder, with a disposition that was vulnerable and sensitive. He was quick to cry at a time when that was certainly not in favor for "real men." My dad was also, at least to my eyes, more than willing to let someone get the best of him in all manner of things. Even though we didn't have much money, he would often loan others money, knowing he was not likely to be repaid.

After living in the rural South for years, he had learned to be resourceful in a place with little to no resources. In the family, we would sometimes refer to him as the mule. He could fix anything, and he would often fix other peoples' cars for free or a promise of future payment, knowing we would not be compensated. It's not that he was unaware of others' intentions, including the intention to take advantage of him, but his approach to life was grounded in love and his faith in God—the God of Christianity. This superseded any other reality.

For years, I was annoyed by this, partially because it pulled me into doing extra work as well. I would often silently side with my mom when she would challenge him for letting people take advantage of him and, by extension, us. I promised myself growing up that I would not be like my father. This is a promise I have broken many times. I now embrace my father's way of living in the world.

I grew up in a full house, full of community and of extended family who opted in because of the love and radiance emanated by my parents. Our story was never one of just struggle—even through the hardest times, there was joy and appreciation.

But my parents and I also had a complicated relationship. I was ruptured from my family for several years as a teenager and young man. And yet I was still loved profoundly. A deep sense of *belonging* was expressed in my family on a daily level. Family is often our early and primary space of belonging. So when that belonging cracked, which would happen when I was eleven, the rupture was painful.

When I say "belonging," what I mean is being seen, knowing that I matter, knowing that I am with people who care deeply about my well-being. Belonging is being a part of something but with the added elements of dignity and even love.

For me belonging was an expression of being home in the deepest sense. In my family, we were all distinct individuals but irreducibly connected. None of us claimed to be just individuals. The unit of understanding would constantly move between the individual and the family. So much so that when my dad wanted to insult me he would say I was an "extreme individual," implying I was disconnected and self-centered.

I am telling you this because our family's rupture and repair were deep lessons in all the dynamics I'll discuss in this book. When a break happens at a core level, especially in our early life or with our most intimate community, it can be very difficult to deal with. But as with much suffering, this fracture within my family also helped shape who I am today, including my understanding of and interest in belonging and the power of bridging. The journey of othering and belonging started early in my life with my family.

We lived in Detroit in a Black community, in a neighborhood often referred to as Black Bottom. My parents, like many Black Americans (still called Negroes then), moved to Detroit as part of the Great Migration of Black people leaving the South, attempting to get away from racial oppression and move toward the promise of opportunity. This migration would land tens of thousands in many northern and western cities in the US, changing the future for thousands of families looking for a world where they could be seen as part of the national fabric and be free of racial terror and violence. This was the attempt to escape the long shadow of enslavement and that peculiar institution that unfortunately, despite incredible progress, still haunts our country today.

While no doubt Detroit in many ways was better than rural Mississippi and Missouri, where my parents had come from, it was still far short of a place where opportunities were open to all. When there were belonging spaces, they were full of conditions and contingencies. Black newcomers were pushed into crowded spaces that often lacked basic services. They were not just segregated from the larger society but segregated from opportunity and often from dignity. While this place still managed to feel teeming with possibilities, like other cities across the country, they were possibilities that would have to, in many ways, be deferred.

My life in Detroit in the 1950s was an almost completely Black world. As a child, I very seldom had contact with any people who weren't Black. I imagined that the world must be largely made of Black people. Of course, we would see white people on television, and people of and in authority were likely to be white—most police, store owners, teachers, and some people who worked at the movie theater, a place I frequented. But most of the people whom I had daily, sustained interaction with were Black.

Yet none of this was particularly salient to my childhood in Detroit. Similar to what writer Zora Neale Hurston noted about not becoming Black, or a colored girl, until she was around white people, for me, growing up in a virtually all-Black working-class community, I was not aware of any other reality. At some level I had no knowledge of Blackness itself. While whiteness was certainly present in knowledge and sometimes physically, being Black as a reference point had not come into clear focus.

This perceptual cocoon I lived in extended across many areas outside of just my family, a reality that would show up later and become influential in who I am. I found very little strange in my first few years of life.

So, for several years, I imagined the world must be largely made of Black people. I was not aware of people from other places, races, or ethnicities. I'd certainly never befriended an immigrant from anywhere. As for Chinese people, whose fate would eventually play a vital role in my path, I'd not only never seen anyone from China, but I was also not aware of any people of any Asian descent. I'm sure there were exceptions, perhaps in restaurants or stores, but these were largely an abstraction.

Despite my physical isolation from other peoples' lives outside of the Black community, I had access to the library and its books, and I had a vivid imagination. From my youngest days I was fiercely curious and was quick to grasp things that I read. I was eager to learn more about the world and its different people, cultures, and places.

All these qualities would set me on an unanticipated course. The new world that opened to me through books would not only change my view of the world, but it would also change my relationship to God, the church, and, most importantly, my family.

The limited geography I traveled, bound as I was in my neighborhood of Black Bottom, was greatly expanded through reading.

When I was eight or nine years old, I picked up a book at the library and started reading about China. Even at that age, it was clear to me that the Chinese people I was reading about were not part of the Christian faith, a fact that would soon collide with my faith and the teachings of the church.

I was raised in the Church of Christ. I didn't join the church; I was born into it. The church to my family was *the* church, not *a* church. It was foundational to our lives. The importance of God and the church to my family's life, and for many years to my life, is hard to overstate.

My father was not just a member of the church—he was a minister in it. When talking to my dad years later about the great love of his life, he without hesitation said the most important love in his life was God. This was followed by my mother and then his children. Knowing the role of faith and of each other in my parents' lives, I did not feel at all slighted by coming in a distant third.

Despite my parents insisting that they loved all nine children the same, we each had our own doubts as to the veracity of this statement. Of course, parents have to say that, but as a child I did not believe it. In my mom's case, each of the nine children privately believed they were the favorite, despite her claims to the contrary. Notwithstanding the story my rational mind tells itself, my heart still feels I am the one most loved by my mother.

So why am I sharing this? Certainly not to make the case that I *was* the most loved. Rather, to share that I held a special place in the family because my own status in the church was of note. While I read a lot in the library, I also read and studied the Bible. I memorized large sections of it. This fact was not missed at church. I was asked to preach sermons by the age of ten, and it was assumed from a very early age that I would grow into a preacher or minister, following in my dad's footsteps. This made the church and my parents extremely proud. This was not just me being good at something; it signaled that I very much believed in our church, the Bible, and the teachings of God. The skills I had were clearly understood to be a gift from God.

It meant that I was destined to carry on God's work. To a deeply religious family, few things could compare.

As I noted, my interest and curiosity were not limited to the Bible. I read about faraway people, places, and even ways of knowing. Reading about China was part of this exploration. What I understood from this reading was not only that most Chinese people were not Christian but that most had probably not heard of Jesus or Christianity.

But what I read about China presented me with a deeply troubling issue. To understand this, you have to know that our church's teaching was that only those baptized in our church denomination, in the name of Jesus, would be saved for eternal life and go to heaven, and all others would be damned for eternity in hell's fire. Belonging, in our church, was extremely conditional. One could be a member only if one accepted the conditions set out by the church. These conditions had come directly from the inspired Bible, so there was no room for compromise or tinkering. These conditions were not negotiable: they were the word of God. This meant that all others who did not adhere to these teachings were going to spend eternity in hell. Only members of the Church of Christ truly belonged. Everyone else was other. This meant that all the Chinese people were going to hell. Even if some Chinese people had heard of Christianity or had become Christians, I did not believe they would likely have heard of the Church of Christ.

For Christians like my family and me, the solution to this was to get the word of the Bible out so that people would hear it and *could* be baptized and saved. While I could rationalize that people, generally speaking, may be afforded some kind of chance to hear the teachings of the Bible to be saved, it seemed clear to me that most Chinese would not have access to these teachings. I developed a deep concern that almost a billion people were going to go to hell simply because they were born on a different part of the earth. I did not understand the thinking that empathy is supposed to be muted by geographical or genetic distance.

This presented a crisis for me that changed my relationship to the church, my family, and myself. I couldn't keep this worry to myself.

One may wonder why an eleven-year-old would be so concerned about these faraway strangers. But at some level I interpreted the teaching of the church to stand for the proposition that *there are no strangers*. We are all the children of God. As an adult, I would still like to believe that.

(To live as if there are no strangers, and indeed to help the stranger, is not just a Christian teaching. At the height of the COVID-19 pandemic, my Muslim neighbors, who knew I lived alone, dropped off a letter on my doorstep. In the letter they asked for my forgiveness. The letter went on to say that the Qur'an calls on Muslims to take care of their neighbors—that there are no strangers. They were concerned and contrite they had not previously lived out this tenet of their beliefs. Their letter was followed by home-cooked meals.)

So in my early concern with the fate of Chinese people, tucked away inside the question "Who are these faraway strangers?" was the question "Who am I?"

I brought the imperative of this inquiry to the church. Every Sunday, following the sermon, the minister at the pulpit would say, "Does anyone have any questions?"

Later I would come to understand that was a rhetorical query. But as an eleven-year-old child, I had an urgent question about these supposed strangers from China, a question that I couldn't find an acceptable answer to on my own. And what does "rhetorical" mean to an eleven-year-old?

One Sunday I raised my hand and stood up when the minister asked his weekly question. As far as I remembered, no one had ever asked a question in my entire childhood in the church. As I stood there, I could feel disapproving gazes and hear an audible collective gasp coming from the congregation.

But Brother Manuel, the minister preaching that day, was kind and inviting. Ignoring the shift and judgment in the congregation, he said, "That's all right, that's all right, Brother powell, what's your question?" Feeling some relief from his openness, I was eager to hear his wisdom. I asked, "Brother Manuel, what's going to happen to the Chinese people?"

He was clearly taken aback. I elaborated. I referred to the teaching that all non-Christians, or—even more to the point—all who did not accept the particular teachings of the Church of Christ, would be condemned to eternal damnation in hell.

This was not what Brother Manuel nor apparently the rest of the church was expecting. He fumbled around for several minutes, flipping through his Bible to try to find some ideas that would help answer my question and assuage my concern. But all the verses he read as possible answers were vague and only made the situation worse. In the end, it was unfortunate, but it seemed that all the Chinese people, including babies and children, including all the good people (for I reasoned there must be good, even innocent, people in China), would be going to hell. The doctrine in my father's church was not that one goes to heaven just for being good. One must be baptized and have one's sin washed away. Being good without this latter part does not address the problem of all people being born in sin. This was how I understood (and still do) the doctrine of the church I was raised in.

That Sunday in church, a day that changed the trajectory of my life, Brother Manuel, after some frustration, dismissed my worries in the best way he knew how. "Don't worry about it," he said. But I did not take his advice. My question was much more than just a worry.

After that day, I never went back to church.

That was the first of a number of profound breaks in my life, and the dynamics of what I call *othering and belonging* began to play out in a life where I had formerly only known belonging. I would go from being sheltered in a cocoon of belonging to being treated as *other* by the people and community I loved the most.

To understand the depth of this break, it's worth noting that the church was not just core to our lives, but irreducible from our lives. While we probably all know people who talk about religion but don't appear to manifest it in their daily lives, that was not the case with my dad. His Christian faith was truly how he experienced his entire life, and our shared faith was what connected our whole family.

While my leaving the church was a defining rupture for the family, it was my father who felt it the most acutely. My father understood church doctrine as follows: if someone fell away from the church, the churchgoers—in their mind, the true believers—were not supposed to have fellowship with that person until and unless they returned to the church. What this meant is that my father and I stopped talking or doing things together. Only conversations that were necessary and functional were had. With one line of questioning, I had gone from being a future preacher to a sinner. For the next four or five painful years, my father and I did not have fellowship. Even as I write this decades later, I can still feel the loss and pain and even wonder or hope that maybe it did not happen. It did.

There was no talking between me and my father for the next several years except in a limited and functional way—to tell me to do my chores and convey other routine matters. On Sundays, the family would head to church, and I would be given a long list of tasks to ensure I wasn't enjoying myself while they were gone.

My mother was conflicted as to how to respond to each of us; she wanted to tend to the pain of her baby boy while also supporting her beloved husband's beliefs.

From this distance, it seems like a very bad movie. And yet this was happening in a family deeply grounded and embedded in love. Navigating this rupture cut down into the heart of how we saw ourselves and one another.

The cut for me went even deeper. My father was not the only one who was deeply religious; I was as well. This break meant I was not just losing relationships with my father, close friends, and my siblings. I was convinced that, like what I had been taught about Chinese people, I was now also condemned to spend eternity living in hell.

So why was I doing this? I do not think I had a choice. I remember in a conversation with God during those years that I acknowledged I was often a sinner and at times even an insufferable, selfish ass. But in this particular case, the matter was not solely about me. I simply could not figure out how to make peace with the condemnation of all these people. It was wrong. I could not be complicit in it, even if it meant standing against God. The contradiction I was holding was that people could be wrong, but not God.

So I was on my own, without my family and without God, at eleven years of age. I was left with a deep sense of aloneness, contradictions, and not knowing the way forward. I had gone from profound belonging to a place of profound other. My place of belonging had not just broken—it had shattered.

It might be too easy to think of the work to heal these ruptures as the start of *john the bridger*. I actually think it was more than that. By necessity, it was the start of *john the searcher*. Having been pushed out of one way of approaching life—suddenly going from being part of an all-encompassing community to not having a community at all—I needed to start searching. For people, yes, and also for some ideas, and for some ways of experiencing the world that made sense to me. I needed an alternative social and spiritual grounding, without knowing if either existed.

My first response to the rupture wasn't to look for ways to heal. I was hurt—and more than hurt, I was confused. I was lonely. When I have shared this story with others as an adult, it's often assumed I must have been so angry and pissed off. But as far as I can recall, this is not accurate. At many levels, I respected my father; I respected him for living his faith, even to the point of abandoning me. Leaving his faith would have meant leaving not only God but himself. As I look back, I can say that I, too, was trying to live my faith and be true to a deeper sense of right and wrong, one that went beyond just my personal concerns and personal comfort.

And yet the break, with not only my parents but all my eleven-year-old self knew, caused suffering in a way that still informs my life. I was very aware of my pain. As a young adult, at times I did not think I would survive. Some people may think of this as a sort of traumatic experience. I cannot say they are wrong, but I can say I don't believe that is how I experienced it then or now. There is suffering that is constitutive and that we can learn from.

It was only much later that I realized my mom and dad were also in pain. While not diminishing their pain, the reality is that they still had the rest of the family as well as their belief in God. Seeing the continued loving family dynamic enjoyed by my siblings, who were still in fellowship with my dad and mom, made it that much more difficult for me to process and navigate this new and strange space with my parents. And being a father myself now, I know that losing one's children, physically or metaphorically, can—with a focus on can—be a very special hurt that may never heal.

Yet out of this suffering and the break with so many core parts of my life, something emerged and was born. I will try to share some of that in the pages that follow. Our suffering can indeed yield many lessons when we are open to receiving or accepting them. I feel fortunate to have had my family, with its radiant love and principled stances, as a model to draw on as I became a bridger.

I never stopped loving my parents. And even through my confusion, I knew they loved me as well. They, and especially my mom, worked as diligently and authentically to hold their love for me as I did for them. Maybe even more so.

As time passed, we reached for one another over and over again. We often missed the mark, but we never gave up on one another. We held onto our loving connection and relationship as solid ground despite our many differences. My father remained deeply committed to his faith. My mom, in her unflappable way, was the main driver who continued to look for bridges between us. She was creative in identifying and constructing new bridges. She would not let go of either her son or her husband. She was determined to have her family back whole.

My parents are both gone now. And I miss them tremendously. Although we each are our own expression of spirit, I have grown to see more consciously and comfortably how much I express my mother and my father. I feel fortunate I had them for as long as I did.

I also feel blessed that we were able to bridge and to heal. It was not an easy process. Through the years that we attempted to find ways back to one another, new breaks would occur and need to be repaired. One such rupture happened around another difference in religious beliefs, a few decades after our break in my childhood. I had been blessed with two wonderful children (a third would come much later). My parents deeply loved children, so this was a cause for celebration. My partner and I made plans to return to Detroit with our two children after being overseas for a spell to spend time with my parents. But my parents told me that I could not share a bedroom with the mother of my children. Why? Because we were not married.

For my parents, their religion dictated that having children outside of marriage was a sin. For me, having left the church as a child, I no longer organized my sense of morality around the concept of sin. This tension was less a question of right and wrong and more an issue of different moral foundations. Trying to respect my parents' values while living my own, I arranged to stay somewhere other than with them. While this solution worked on some level, we were all pained nonetheless. Afterward, each subsequent trip back to Detroit was marred by the injury of this first visit.

After some years of this arrangement, I received a letter from my mother. In the letter, she stated that she had witnessed my love and devotion to my partner and my children. She had decided that regardless of what the law said, she believed in the eyes of God that I was married. She invited my family and me to stay with her and my father from here on out.

I am sharing this because it was a wonderful lesson and a deep expression of love. It speaks to my mother's deep commitment to finding ways for us to heal and to bridge, to the loving and skillful work she initiated to find ways to keep us together.

This was the last major break I had with my parents. There was no lingering residue left after our reconciliation. There was nothing left unsaid or love left unexpressed.

I am telling these stories about how I've learned to bridge from them, and from our breaking with each other, as part of my own practice of faith and hope for the future. I don't come at this just from an intellectual place or from being an academic; I come to this in large part by way of being a child of my parents, as well as a spiritual being. The spirit in me remains curious, moved by the wonders of life, and the knowing and the not knowing that go beyond the intellect and are anchored in love and belonging.

My mother died first, and then my dad died about twenty years later. I often say my mother taught me to love individuals up close. My dad taught me to love humanity and life. I am still learning.

1

Bridging to the Future

This book is about four key concepts paired in tension with each other: *belonging* and *bridging* and *othering* and *breaking*. I'll go into much greater detail to define each of these and how they are interrelated, but let me offer some brief introductions now to what I mean by these four words.

I believe many of our most vexing social problems share a common structure that is not often revealed when we are just looking at single issues. I believe that the concept of *othering*, or seeing people not only as different but as less deserving and not of equal dignity as us, allows us to more clearly perceive the underlying structure of many of the problems we are facing, whether we call those problems racism, nationalism, homophobia, or cancel culture.

Breaking is othering in action. When we engage in breaking, we deny the full stories, complexities, and even sometimes the humanity of those we consider other. Their suffering does not count as much as ours. While othering is about one's status in relationship to different groups, breaking is the practice that undergirds othering.

The solutions that I want to offer to othering and breaking are belonging and bridging.

Belonging serves as an aspiration and orientation in the world. A world built on belonging means one must have what is necessary to cocreate and participate in making the world one lives in. Belonging means agency for all members of society. It is closely associated with dignity and being seen. While in a sense we already belong, it is still important that we are acknowledged as belonging and that we acknowledge the belonging of others.

At a foundational, and I would say spiritual, level, belonging also means that *there is no other*. Whose life is unimportant? Who does not matter? Show me the person not made of stardust. Not only do we all count, but we are all connected. *We all belong*.

And yet that is not our daily experience. We are situated differently from others. We see the world differently from others. How am I to be my brother's and sister's keeper when they see the world so differently than I do? Maybe they even reject the idea that they are my brother or sister. There are many practices, like in my father's church, willing to embrace the notion that all the members belong but not the nonmembers—not the Chinese people, or the eleven-year-old who questioned the rules of belonging. Othering may seem natural and even inevitable. It is neither. But we must do something in a world where we practice not seeing the humanity in the other.

This is where bridging comes in.

Bridging is both a practice and a position. "Can I become a bridge?" I may ask myself. And this immediately calls up other questions— "Do I want to bridge?" Or "Why should I?"

By definition, if someone is other, there is apparently a distance between us. Why don't I just leave it at that? Maybe they are more than different—maybe they are a threat. Should I bridge or should I protect myself from this other?

We live in a world full of fractures and one where polarization, division from one another, and isolating ourselves are becoming increasingly normalized. We live in a world where fear is often more visible than love or hope.

But it does not have to be that way. In our effort to protect ourselves in what feels like a dystopian world, to close ourselves off from one another, we are likely to inflict even more pain and add fuel to the fire of the very world we want to avoid.

This book suggests there is another way. This book hopes to acknowledge and reclaim our ability to see one another. And to live with one another.

Where there is an apparent other, there is the need to explore how to bridge. This book is about belonging *without* othering despite the claim that the world demands something else. This book is an invitation to reject a future organized around fear and death, and instead to organize and call into being a world where we recognize and live into our connection with one another, the earth, and ourselves. It is known that we share much DNA with apes. What is less discussed is that we also share DNA with all of life. To live into this reality of interbeing is the challenge.

This is not an easy task, and there will be many reasons to think and do otherwise. And yet, life demands life, and I believe bridging is one of our most important ways to see and celebrate one another and ourselves.

The Power of Stories

A slightly different approach to the four concepts I have named would be to ask: "How do we move from a world built on breaking and othering to one built on bridging and belonging?"

One way is through stories.

What do stories have to do with bridging? Stories are vital to the human experience. Indeed, a more fundamental question may be "What do stories have to do with us?" Stories are what help us make sense of the world and ourselves. We are meaning-making animals, and stories are the tools we use to make meaning.

There is strong evidence that we do not have a coherent sense of ourselves until we develop a story about ourselves. When we remember the past or we anticipate the future, it is largely through stories.

Anthropologist Clifford Geertz stated that all knowledge is local, made and held by communities who share experiences, understandings, and expectations with one another. That knowledge is carried in our stories, which in turn shape our world and give it meaning. While some of our stories may appear individual, they are always embedded in a social community, bound up with the community's set of stories. Indigenous knowledge and history is irreducible from the stories that are told about the world that anchor community in past, present, and future. For more on this see the work of scholars Robin Wall Kimmerer (Potawatomi) and Patty Krawec (Anishnaabe).

Different societies and different eras have different stories. Some cultures think of time as circular; some think of it as linear. The point is not that one group or perspective is right and another one wrong; the point is that our lives and relationships are shaped by these different stories.

We all carry multiple stories, as well as multiple selves, something I'll return to later. When I first met the Buddhist teacher Joanna Macy, she said, "john, tell me your story." I responded, "Joanna, as you know, we have many stories, and none are completely true or accurate." Joanna replied, "Of course. Just pick one."

I sometimes hesitate to share my own personal stories for several reasons. One is not wanting to be overly identified with a single story. But another reason is because I know that we hear other people's stories against a backdrop of our *own* story, as well as of the larger story that society carries. When this happens, my own complex story often gets missed.

As a relatively successful Black man in America, I often experience an overweighted interest in a *single* story about my life. There is a tendency to make my Blackness my entire story—or, conversely, to assert it is not consequential at all. I remember being with a wonderful white friend in Minneapolis who asked me what it is like to be a Black man in Minneapolis, which at that time was one of the whitest cities in the United States. When I turned the question back to her and asked what it was like to be a white person in Minneapolis, she was puzzled. Her experience of whiteness in Minneapolis was so pervasive, she had no distance to allow her to look at it. Like me as a child in Detroit, surrounded by Blackness I didn't see, she was living with whiteness all around, and therefore it was invisible. In a sense I can know Blackness only when I have some distance from it or it is in relationship to something else.

The other story is that my race does not matter at all. Some people will insist that being a "good" person means we don't see one another's race, gender, or other descriptive category, that our individuality and spirit cannot be reduced to any category. And while it is true we cannot be reduced, it is also a false hope that we are not touched by these categories or that we can remain unaware they exist. Being Black is not my whole story, but neither is the story of me being an individual "I."

The first story has often come with an invitation for me to share stories of how I "overcame." To me there is tacit in that request yet another story, one about the others who did *not* overcame. So an apparently positive story about me—that is, how I became successful—reflects a not-so-positive story about others who were not only less fortunate but maybe, in the mind of the person hearing my story, less deserving.

This story itself—how we are self-made, how we can individually overcome our family history, life circumstances, and the structures and contexts we live in—is part of a larger story in the United States. And I believe that larger story is not only distorting and incomplete but also at times harmful. I don't know who I, john, am without my parents or my family, without the experiences that shaped how I see the world and who I am in and to the world. Even from my earliest story, there was no me without a larger we.

As I suggested in the preface, when I share the story of my parents, the listener often inserts their own story about how difficult my parents' lives must have been, given the social and material status of Black Americans of their generation. This assumption distorts much of the larger meaning of what it was like growing up in my family. This simplistic story misses who I am and how I experience my life.

As I share more stories throughout the book, both about myself and about others, I will strive to make all of them as accurate as possible, especially the ones about myself. And yet I have no doubt that when I describe my eleven-year-old self or my fifty-year-old self, what I experienced then and how I made meaning of it then are not the same as how I remember it today.

This is in part because when we remember, it is not simply a *recall* of what happened. We are constantly reinterpreting our past and the meaning behind its events. I am not talking about fabrication or deceit. But even in our clearest and most deliberate efforts, we cannot get to a story about ourselves, or the world, without being shaped by things that often lie largely beyond our cognitive grasp, such as metaphors and language. There are parts of our lives that are just not fully available to us without meanings assigned changing over time.

And yet too often we leave little room for doubt, uncertainty, and change about our stories. We have all witnessed people who are very close, people with long histories together, trying to agree on a small or large event in their life, yet agreement frequently eludes them. They remember the same event differently, with different implications.

This is even more pronounced when we are looking beyond facts to find *meaning*. When I think of my own life, I am aware there are many stories, and their meanings are still emerging. And I experience my memories and meaning making afresh as I myself grow and change. So this is not just about what something *did* mean but also about what *it will mean* in the future. This meaning making will be in part filtered through a language and culture that the "individual" is born into and can never completely control.

The world is not here solely to be observed. We are very much a part of this world and are constantly reinterpreting ourselves and our story in it. In a society like the United States, informed by Christian religion, for example, even those who are non-Christian or secular will find their lives and cultural cues to be deeply informed by Christian concepts. For example, the concepts of sin and redemption or of good and evil will have meaning for most people in the West in a way that would likely not register to someone from a society grounded in a different religious tradition or foundation.

We are not separate from each other or separate from the world. The claim of connectedness may seem counterintuitive and even strange to those of us raised on the myth of our separation from nature and each other and the need to dominate others and the earth.

But it is the claim of separation that is strange, not to say fear inducing. The other often represents a fear, the threat of what is unknown and uncertain. This fear creates the need to dominate or domesticate. We love the domesticated, manicured park but remain fearful of the uncontrollable nature of the forest.

But uncertainty and unknowing are not just lurking out there or in the other; they are part of our very being. Earlier, I wrote about not having a single story and having uncertainty about my story and experience. Some may find my claims of a multiplicity of selves or uncertainty around memory disturbing. They may also just flat out disagree. Rather than presenting an obstacle, though, I believe this space of uncertainty can be a space of hope for bridging and belonging.

It may also provide the space for the other. Significant research in the science of cognition indicates that much of life and how we perceive it is full of uncertainty and gaps.

While the hope for certainty may be understandable, the reality we are forced to live with is anything but.

This insight around the certainty of uncertainty is not a problem; indeed, the reality of our fluidity and multiplicity is one of the ways that we can support bridging. Bridging recognizes the need for a larger and unfolding story that holds our aspirations for a shared future based on belonging, not fear and separation. This story is one both of facts and of meaning. This is not only a never-ending story but a never-complete story.

Not having perfect clarity with others or ourselves about the past at a *personal* level takes on a much sharper relief at a *societal* level, and often with much higher and more material stakes. Institutions and the state also have stories and histories but hold greater power than individuals to enforce or ignore stories, a subject I'll get into more deeply throughout this book.

The world of stories does not always line up with the real world, and yet the imagined world of our stories—not only about our past but also about what we tell ourselves about the future—has importance in the real world. Historian and philosopher Yuval Noah Harari finds the *ability to imagine* to be one of the unique gifts bestowed on humans that allows us to create new things and, equally important, allows us to build a bridge to a future where we can make a larger *us*. Bridging helps us build *practices* to imagine a shared story for the future rooted in belonging for all humans and the earth, too.

Bridging is about the emerging story of moving toward *us and us*, not *us versus them*. In *bridging stories*, the lines and boundaries are constantly being renegotiated. In *breaking stories*, some voices are muted or distorted for the benefit of one group and not the other. While bridging stories embrace the nuance of the truth, breaking stories are more likely to embrace the simplicity of a lie.

Bridging and breaking are not simply a binary. Many breaks are not complete breaks, and many bridges are not complete bridges. Bridging is more of an orientation and compass than a destination.

That's why in this book I will be calling on both stories and our imagination to talk about the power of bridging. And while understanding bridging and belonging helps us make sense of the moment we are in, they are also about creating possibility and a story for the future.

I hope that my sharing some versions of stories, both my own and those of our larger society, helps to convey my journey of becoming a *bridger* and may provide some guidance to you on yours.

The Urgency of Bridging

Why do I believe (and I do believe) this work of bridging is urgent? Because we are living right now in a world where there is a great deal of fragmentation. This is often framed as *polarization* and sometimes as *isolation*, or both. While these three dynamics are related, I believe *fragmentation* is a better way of understanding and addressing our current state.

Polarization is usually defined by two sides diverging in roughly symmetrical ways, with the implication being that to solve polarization everyone can moderate their positions and meet in a perceived middle. That may sound appealing, but often it is not the correct solution. What about a case where one side embraces steps to avert impending disaster while the other is not only entrenched in inaction but denies there is even an issue? Not all instances of groups diverging should or even *can* be resolved by negotiating a middle position.

I prefer the term *fragmentation* to describe the widespread dynamic of retreat into groups that are mutually averse to and distrustful of each other. To address fragmentation, we must also understand and address power and contexts of different groups, while at the same time anchoring our efforts in values that include *all* people.

Social division, fragmentation, and isolation are all global issues and are a threat to the health of democracy and the planet. We should be careful in both analysis and language about them. (I write more about fragmentation in the book *Racing to Justice*.)

Fragmentation and distrust are on the rise. In the US, the gap between how positively individuals feel toward others of their own political party versus members of the opposing political party has grown steadily since the early 1990s. By 2020, animosity toward the opposing political party was at its highest point in decades, as measured by a public opinion survey tool called the "feeling thermometer," which asks Americans to rate how warm or cold they feel toward different groups, including those in different political parties.

In 2022, an NBC News survey showed that 80 percent of people with political affiliations believed the other party "poses a threat that if not stopped will destroy America as we know it." This was shown to be in part because Americans exaggerate how different they are from supporters of the other party, and therefore they carry in their heads distorted and flattened stories of one another. The less we meaningfully interact across differences—the less we stay open to *bridging*—the more likely that such stories become a reality.

There is distrust not just of the apparent *other* but of each other, even those we may think of as members of our group. This is sometimes expressed in terms of social isolation and loneliness. The British government noted loneliness as a national problem and appointed a minister of loneliness to help address it. The US Surgeon General has issued warnings that we are in an epidemic of loneliness.

People are experiencing not just increased loneliness but also anger, hopelessness, and little faith in institutions. A 2023 survey from the Public Religion Research Institute (PRRI) found that more than three-quarters of Americans believe that our democracy is at risk in the 2024 US presidential election. And 38 percent agreed with the statement that "because things have gotten so far off track, true American patriots may have to resort to violence in order to save our country," the highest rate of support for political violence in the eight surveys PRRI has conducted since 2021.

All over the world, an increasing number of people are facing the future with a mix of anxiety, fear, and trepidation. These feelings are a breeding ground for authoritarianism and worse. Peace-building organizations globally are being challenged to reconsider their values and their approach as wars in Ukraine, Sudan, and Gaza rage on. Even those who may conceptually support building bridges between different groups worry it may be a luxury we cannot afford in this environment.

So why are war and othering increasing now, and why all over the world?

One reason is because the world is changing rapidly, and rapid change puts us under enormous pressure, straining our ability to adapt. Today's accelerated changes are happening across critical areas that have enormous impact on all of us—climate crisis, technological advances, economic shifts, the COVID pandemic, and altering demographics all portend a different world. The speed of these changes will not likely slow down.

These dynamics are raising Darwinian narratives, such as *who will survive* and *who will fit in this emerging new world*. While the reference to Darwin might seem abstract, the experience is anything but. We frequently respond to the challenge of change by finding a target to assuage our anxiety. And too often that target becomes the other. It can be the racial other, the immigrant other, the trans other. As Darwin discussed survival of the fittest, he appeared to be discussing traits and species. The application and use in social discourse may not align completely with Darwinian theory of the survival of the fittest, but that will not likely have much impact on either the discussion or the underlying anxiety.

There are indeed changes coming. The future, somewhat like the past, is complex, only more so. The changes may be scary, or they may be something we believe we want. But they all point to a world where we will all be called upon to change. What is most fearful is the possibility that my group, and I, will not belong in this new world.

Even if we don't want to change, change is inevitable. It might be good, bad, both, and neither. But life does not exist without change. The change could be slow enough that we don't notice it, but when change is too fast, it may appear to threaten our current way of being. Our sense of threat may feel even more troubling when we begin to allow the belief that the unwelcome change is being caused by an other.

People are navigating these changes without much help from leaders and without stories that can support them in meeting the moment with something other than fear. Changing US immigration policies or leaving the European Union is not likely to address the issue of climate or demographic changes. And people are not likely to invest in serious solutions for any number of causes unless such solutions speak to some real concerns that impact their daily lives. The energy we see around book bans in schools suggests that it might be easier to get people excited about what their children are reading or not reading than about issues like climate change or artificial intelligence, which might feel more removed and abstract.

The collective anxiety that we are experiencing due to the pace of change in the world today can be met with fear and more anxiety, or it can be met by creating opportunities to turn toward one another and build a larger *we* that can face the future together.

I believe bridging is one such opportunity.

Bridging is a powerful way to address fragmentation and create a shared story for our future. I believe understanding the threats of othering and the orientation of belonging will help us meet the future with the urgency we need.

The Role of Stories in Our Changing World

The role of stories is vital in all these dynamics. And I believe right now there are three stories, or some combination of them, that can be told.

The first story is that there is no real change happening and everything will continue to be just like it is. It is offered to address fears by insisting that there will not be any significant change. This is the least credible story, even if it is often employed.

The second story is that we are heading for a future where things could get much worse. Who we are, our very way of life, are up for grabs. If we do not do something quick—and possibly something extreme—it will be too late. You may read this as a warning about climate change. It could be, but in this story it's not climate change that accelerates the anxiety for many. The central factor that shapes our anxiety is about the *other*. The dreaded other is put forth as the most immediate and profound threat to our way of life and our very existence. As our anxiety searches for a target, the demagogue is more than willing to point to a marginal other as the source.

In this story, we hear *they* are threatening *us*—they are taking our jobs, they are bringing crime to our communities, they are importing strange religious practices to our neighborhood. In this story they threaten who we are. This threat at some level may even portend extinction: we may die, or we may be replaced, or we may be changed so much as to be unrecognizable. Sometimes this reads as the possibility that our collective group purity will be polluted. We will become strangers in our own land. Unless we act now, we are really f*cked.

The zombies and the vampires are at the gates, and the elites are with them. There is no room in this story for the possibility that we might live together. Attacks and other forms of violence can be recast as self-defense and the protection our group.

Then there is the third story. The third story is also one of change. But the change is good or at least it is potentially good. In this story there is a future where all of us belong. In this story we will be a more diverse and more connected people. We will learn to listen to each other and contribute our unique histories and realities. We will turn toward each other, instead of on each other, and we will work together to create structures and societies where we can all participate, celebrating our differences instead of pretending we are all the same.

I believe the second and third stories are likely to be the dominant stories of the rest of the century.

The second story is what I call a breaking story. It tells of a smaller and smaller we in constant struggle with the threatening other. This story is deeply motivated by fear and limited imagination. This story has currency all over the globe and is growing in circulation and scale. Adherents to any version of the second story are, even if unconsciously, afraid of the future and may wish to retreat to a mythical past. Some common themes in this story are ethnic purity, domination, and the building of boundaries and structures to keep us apart.

The third story is a bridging story. It tells the story of a larger and larger we, with an aspiration that there is no other and an intention to work to build practices and relationships that support that aspiration. This larger we need not become an undifferentiated we. There is still the need for expressions of multiple groups. Belonging is not treating everyone as the same.

Bridging is a story rooted in belonging, where the we is reconstituted, where everyone has the agency to shape the world we live in. Yes, the world will be different. Yes, we will be different. But we will find new ways to connect. Even though we may appear different to one another, we will recognize and live the fact that we have more in common than we do differences and can create new commonalities.

And if we embrace this recognition, the we of the future will be not only larger but better. We will still have differences, but the boundaries between us will be more porous.

The bridging story is one of a cocreated future where bridges instead of walls are the norm. It is a story of shared faith—in each other and in our future.

In some sense, the groups from the second and third stories want the same things: a world where they are safe, their fears are quieted, and their concerns are considered. A world where they belong. But they believe different things and practices will deliver this future or move them closer to it.

Both the breaking story and the bridging story are about belonging. The breaking story is focused on only one group's belonging and this belonging being threatened by the other. (It is the ethnic cleansing that is discussed in Michael Mann's book *The Dark Side of Democracy*.) It is making the nascent US "safe" for Europeans by cleansing it of Native Americans. The breaking group believes this safe world is in the past, where if there is an other, they are dominated and controlled for the benefit of the legitimate we. The bridging group, on the other hand, leans toward a future where we are safe only when the world and our stories support our interconnection and mutuality.

For those of you ready to engage in the future, I have good news. It is coming. For those of you who would prefer to stay in the past, the news is not as good.

Much of what happens in the emerging future—not all, but much—depends on us. I believe that future is worth living and the road to that future is one of bridging and belonging. We cannot imagine a future where we all belong unless we can learn to bridge.

While I will go into some depth about the challenges we are facing, this is not a book about despair. I am not a person who is prone to that emotion. But neither am I a person who organizes solely around hope. It has been said that hope alone is not a strategy. But when we do things together, possibilities indeed become countless. Bridging is one of those possibilities.

I believe we in the United States have been on a journey from the time of our formation as a nation, when our practices started with a very small *we* living in an exclusionary society, moved toward a partially integrated society, progressed further to an inclusive society, and now, I posit, are growing toward a belonging society.

The original "We the People" clause in the US Constitution conceived of a very small we. Enslaved people were not included in that we, women were not included in that we, men without property were not included, Indigenous people were not included, nonwhite immigrants were excluded, and so on. By some accounts, fewer than one-sixth of adults were included in the we at the founding of the United States.

Other nations and regions have had similar arcs. A few hundred years ago, most of Europe—indeed much of the world—did not consider most people to fully count or belong as members of the we. Belonging was reserved for royalty and the aristocratic classes.

Many of the debates we're having today are about *who belongs*. As demands for the we to grow have generated expansion, there has also been contraction. Genocide and ethnic cleansing are explicit assertions and practices around the notion that some people, including former members and current inhabitants, are now not part of the we and do not belong. Narratives about groups assigned to the nonbelonging space are then widely circulated—that they are to be feared, controlled, and maybe even destroyed. In 2022, Viktor Orbán, the prime minister of Hungary, asserted that Hungary is a country for white Europeans only, where people of color do not belong.

So can we imagine a future where *all* belong? I believe we not only can, we must. But only together.

This book is meant to help us cultivate the practices that can guide us toward that future and toward a new story where no person is left out of our circle of concern.

While this could be read as an optimistic view of the future, I am not optimistic nor pessimistic. I refer to myself as a *possibilist*. I believe life and the world are full of contingencies, and what we do and do not do matter. We cannot know how life will treat us, but the best chance of having an impact is not to control the unknown, but to engage the possibilities. We are not helpless, especially if we can act and cocreate together. That is how I try to live this life.

I introduced the concepts of bridging and breaking in the sharing of my stories as a boy growing up in Detroit and my break with my parents. I will continue to return to some of these lessons throughout this book.

I think a deeper dive into the meanings of the terms I'm offering here—*othering, breaking, belonging,* and *bridging*—is necessary, as these are deceptively simple terms with many layers. I will try to peel off some of the layers. The purpose of the book is not just to define these terms but to demonstrate why belonging and bridging are necessary in our increasingly broken world, as well as to point us in the direction of how we might begin to orient ourselves toward them in our own lives.

At the core of bridging is the willingness to stay open and to recognize the inherent humanity of all people. The attitude we bring to bridging is more crucial than any specific steps we might learn on how to bridge. Indeed, how we bridge will look different in different situations, and it will continue to change.

As you read through this book and contemplate your own relationship with bridging, I offer some questions for reflection at the end of each chapter. I encourage you to sit with those—even more, perhaps to write them down and talk about them with others. Engage in conversations about these questions and about bridging. From experience, I have seen much of the most robust bridging work being done today in dialogue with other people. It is useful to grapple with the questions and feelings that arise as we practice bridging as part of our aspiration to move toward a world where all belong and none are othered.

This is the charge of belonging, and this is my charge in life. I hope it is or may become yours.

So let's get on with it.

Reflect

- What story do you tell yourself about the inevitable change in the world? Is it good? Bad? Something more complex?

- Where in your life do you feel you belong?

- Where do you feel you don't belong? Where do you feel like you are *other*?

- Who to you is *other* and why?

- Do you *other* some parts of your self?

- Can you imagine a world where everyone belongs? What might it look like?

2

The Problem Is Othering

L et's start with the problem. Understanding the problem can help
us better understand the need for the solutions as well as sharpen
our examination of the problem.

In my writings and public life, I have frequently asserted that *the
problem of the twenty-first century is the problem of othering*. In this
assertion, I am consciously playing off the work of the great American
public intellectual and author W. E. B. Du Bois, who declared over
one hundred years ago that "the problem of the Twentieth Century is
the problem of the color-line."

Forty years after Du Bois wrote those words, the Swedish scholar
Gunnar Myrdal characterized the race problem in the United States as
a great dilemma that, if not resolved, threatened the ultimate success
of our democratic experiment. Indeed, as I write these words, it seems
we may be abandoning this grand experiment.

I am asserting that the key problem both Myrdal and Du Bois
were grappling with was *othering*. And I am also asserting that
belonging without othering is the way to address othering. It is
not enough to create belonging for one group while creating and
intensifying othering for another. I believe that understanding more
about how othering works will help us comprehend why bridging
and belonging are such powerful responses to combat it.

The other and *othering* have long been applied as scholarly terms, such as in postcolonialism (see Edward Said's 1978 book *Orientalism*, with regard to the racial othering of Middle Eastern and Asian communities) and in gender and sexuality studies (see Simone de Beauvoir's 1949 *The Second Sex*, on women in a patriarchal society). The terms *othering* and *belonging* do not each have a single or simple definition, but perhaps we should not be surprised about that. Any time we try to define a core concept, like equality or even love, we quickly find that there is no single definition, and we know intuitively the concept is more opaque than we thought.

As James Baldwin noted, "Words like 'freedom,' 'justice,' 'democracy' are not common concepts; on the contrary, they are rare. People are not born knowing what these are."

Take the concept of *equality*, the meaning of which has been continuously contested in our society. As historian Darrin M. McMahon writes in his book *Equality: The History of an Elusive Idea*, equality's elusiveness means it is constantly being made and remade.

The US Supreme Court has made numerous efforts to ground what the Constitution means by "equality" into law. They try to look back in time to discern what the drafters of the Constitution meant by "equality." Many Supreme Court justices have asserted that *their* interpretation is the true definition of equality as reflected in the Constitution, yet they strongly disagree with how various people or groups apply the concept of equality. They often come up with very different stories, with radically different meanings, of what this important concept meant then and means now.

Lack of agreement between members of the highest court of the United States can quickly be extended to other important concepts that shape our lives, such as free speech or race, to name a couple. How the Supreme Court understands and addresses the question of equality, as well as other concepts, has major implications for the entire country. The power of the justices lies not in their credentials, but in how they take up these core issues that have an impact on our society, our stories, and our future. We need not be disturbed that there is no single clear meaning of "equality." The concern is when justices and pundits act as if there *is* a single, fixed meaning, and it is the one they are applying.

I will try not to make this mistake with the four central concepts of this book. I will not define them in simple or singular ways; rather, I will go deeper into how I am using these terms and try to work toward a common understanding. I recognize that others might approach these terms quite differently than I do. In this book, and in my work, I am sharing *a* definition or approach, not *the* definition or approach.

Why Othering (and Not Race)?

To understand more clearly how I define *othering*, it may be instructive to also look at other frames we use to define marginalization and inequality. One common question I am asked when I talk about *othering*, especially in the US, is: Why do I not focus on race and racism instead?

As someone who has worked for decades in the civil rights and civil law field, and as a teacher of structural racialization, I don't find this question unexpected. The reality is that in the US (but not only the US) housing, education, school, and health care, as well as whose stories are told or not, are all deeply organized around race. To get an idea of that one has only to look at the number of books and articles trying to understand and address the central inequality of race that seems to be pressing in our society.

In one such book, *Racial Formation in the United States*, considered a landmark work on race, scholars Michael Omi and Howard Winant called race the master narrative for understanding formative social gaps in American society. Their work posited, with a substantial body of empirical findings, that in the US the primary social schism is related to race, revealing how racism helps make sense of all other social challenges. Omi and Winant argued that race as a phenomenon does not just define the other group but is critical for how the dominant white group constitutes *itself*.

A number of people today increasingly accept that there is no scientific basis for race. This is not just an abstract thought. This line of thinking lies behind much of the Supreme Court's reasoning for adopting, and I would say misapplying, colorblindness. The reasoning goes something like this: If race and racism are not real, an intelligent or good person will not see race. They will be race blind.

Many who look carefully at race often agree that it is not a biological reality but a *social* reality. These social realities have real life implications and cannot simply be wished away. Race as a biological or scientific construct need not exist for racism as a social phenomenon to be quite real.

An important question then becomes: If race is *not* biologically determined, what are the social conditions that create and maintain race and racism? If it is not biological, then we must accept that we have collectively created race and racism.

The reality is much more nuanced. Even though race is not a scientific fact, many important things we believe and which guide our lives are not scientific. Many people assert that God or the divine are not scientifically proven. Many assert that the self as understood in Western society is a myth, a fiction. Yet this does not lessen the impact these beliefs have on people. The US Constitution is explicit in protecting and respecting various religious identities and practices. Should it matter that there are no scientific bases for these religions? One could continue along these lines. What are the scientific bases for our national identities? Even posing the questions may sound strange. And yet, given how we distribute resources on the basis of national identities, such identities are individually and socially very important.

One of this book's central points is that the other is not scientifically or otherwise a given. There is no natural other. But there are others who are constituted sociologically, and the impact of that is very real. It should be clear that whether something has a scientific basis or not doesn't always determine how we respond.

Unfortunately, many who may accept the truth of race not being a scientific fact do not explore the social phenomena behind racism.

It is a worthy exploration, and while I have written about this in depth (especially in *Racing to Justice*), for the purposes here of discussing race related to othering and belonging, I will say that racism is not something just created by prejudiced or bad individuals. Racial categories must be socially created and given meaning prior to the experience of individual prejudice. The process of constructing race is complicated and multifaceted. (For more, see *Making Race and Nation* by Anthony W. Marx, who looks at the history of race and nation making in the US, South Africa, and Brazil; and *Rules of Racialization* by Steve Martinot.)

In the 1960s, the landmark National Advisory Commission on Civil Disorders, known as the Kerner Commission, conducted one of the largest studies ever done on race and inequality in the US. The presidentially appointed commission noted that America was moving toward two separate societies: one black and one white, separate and unequal. The commission articulated these dynamics to attempt to bring understanding to the deep divisions in our society. Racism and separation were found to be threatening the very health and survival of our society. To deny the humanity of large groups of people is harmful not only to the targeted other but also to the dominant group.

It is important to note here that there is no natural other. Racism can be organized around features that are real or imagined. Yet simply acknowledging that a category has a constructed foundation does not detract from the very real consequences of a category being imposed. Nor does it suggest that we can just wish categories away. Most people today may say that witches and the devil are not real threats, and yet millions of people died for being witches or for being under the influence of the devil.

So, while it is not unusual for people to accept that race is not a biological reality or to state that race is not real, racism and the effects of having a *race* or being *raced* are quite real.

The state does not just distribute resources, it distributes identities and makes groups as well. Consider the question of what groups in our society have legal recognition and protection. Is homosexuality a natural condition or a chosen one? This is largely a question that has been undertaken by the state. As far as I know, a similar question about heterosexuality has never been asked.

When the US became a nation, one of the first laws the federal government passed was that only white people could immigrate here and become US citizens. But what constituted "white" was largely left up to individual states. Some states defined "white" as not having any Black blood, the so-called "one drop rule." Some states adopted a rule that a person who was more than one-sixteenth Black could not be white. The early focus of the law was largely on the axis of Black and white, so much so that some early laws defined people of Chinese descent as Black. All these classifications were related to what the state afforded or did not afford to these categories. There were benefits attached to who was classified as white and deficits associated with those who were classified as not white.

Let me share a few more poignant examples of the state's power to define and divide groups. In the early twentieth century, Bhagat Singh Thind was an Asian Indian immigrant who raised a family and started a successful business in the US. As he got older, he wanted to become a naturalized citizen of the US—the place he considered home and where he had built his life. But he was not granted citizenship upon applying in 1919. His efforts to become a citizen then went all the way to the US Supreme Court. Thind argued to the court that he was a white person from India—and not only white, but part of the original white race. To be white signaled he was deserving of American citizenship. The court rejected his claim and stated that regardless of the scientific meaning of white, in American society he would never be accepted as white. His request for citizenship was denied. Afterward another Indian man, Vaishno Bagai, who had his citizenship revoked as a result of the Thind case, committed suicide.

Another way to look at race is that it is not just about physiology of skin color but also about status. I turn to James Baldwin for his insight. When talking about whiteness, Baldwin asserted that there is no hope for white people as long as they feel whiteness is an essential feature of their lives. He was not talking about the physical appearance of (phenotypical) whiteness, but about the meaning and status that the idea of whiteness confers. He was also talking about the constitution of the very categories of white and Black, meaning, "As long as you think you're white, I'm going to be forced to think I'm Black."

The assertion that President Barack Obama was not a "real" American was bound up with the assumption that real Americans are white Christians. Former 2024 Republican presidential hopeful Governor Nikki Haley (born Nimarata Nikki Randhawa) is of Indian ancestry but was not painted with the same story that she is not a real American and therefore not eligible to be president, likely because many people think she physically appears to be white.

There also exists the position that some groups are white-adjacent. Asian Americans have long been classified as the "model minority." This seemingly positive statement is actually problematic and has been rejected by many Asian American groups and individuals. The US has had a long and ambivalent history of trying to situate Asians in the American lexicon of race, particularly in relationship to whiteness and Blackness. This designation is not just descriptive; it allocates social status and rights. Whiteness has been associated with the right to become a naturalized citizen, to vote, and, most importantly, to belong. Asian Americans, because they are regarded as white-adjacent, will sometimes be accorded that status of whiteness. Society does this in part to make a negative statement about Black Americans but also to grant some provisional rights.

These claims are not harmless. There is the continued assumption in the US that whites are deserving and people of color and immigrants are not. In America, whiteness is associated with belonging and nonwhiteness with a special role. It is important to note these categories were nuanced. There were whites, and then there were Irish and Eastern Europeans.

The relevant point for this conversation is that these categorizations are created largely by the state, not individuals. The concept of race helped to *create* the very racial identities the state was attempting to regulate. (For those who would like to look more deeply at these issues, I recommend *White by Law* by Ian Haney Lopez, *How the Irish Became White* by Noel Ignatiev, and *The Invention of the White Race* by Theodore W. Allen.)

The functioning of a race-based system did not require those labeled white, Black, or otherwise to agree. Even by the 1960s several states still outlawed interracial marriage between Black and white Americans. In prohibiting interracial marriages, the state used police and the law to enforce racial segregation. Richard Loving, the white husband in *Loving v. Virginia,* the Supreme Court case that challenged antimiscegenation laws, was arrested and spent time in jail for being married to a Black woman. Loving's whiteness was also called into question by his association with the racial *other*. This insight is often lost: our membership in a group can be compromised by associating with some outside our group.

The Benefits of Focusing on Othering

This brings us back to why I focus on othering instead of focusing solely on racism.

Many people, including a growing number today, believe that races are naturally in conflict when in close contact with each other, and therefore races must be segregated to have a sustained peaceful existence. The doctrine of *separate but equal* was built on this assumption. It is not clear what that would mean exactly or how it would be accomplished.

Some try to ground this idea of natural separation in genes, others in religious texts, and still others in social and cultural practices. This belief in the inherent difference between groups is not stable.

A number of racial justice activists are concerned that a focus on othering will take attention away from anti-Black racism work. (An unstated assumption exists that talking about race in the US is about a Black-versus-white frame.) This concern is understandable given that in the US today, politicians continually make an effort to avoid talking about racism while leaving many racialized practices and norms in full effect. Some political leaders in the US generally would be all too eager to stop everyone from talking about race, yet are not disturbed by wealth, housing, or health care segregation by race.

We see both a hypersensitivity to race *and* an effort to redefine or even erase our history of race. We are currently witnessing efforts to deny the history of slavery or to turn slavery into a positive thing for those who were enslaved. Some states are limiting teaching about slavery; diversity, equity, and inclusion (DEI); critical race theory; structural racism; and more. A current claim is that enslavement happened a long time ago and we should get over it. Part of the rationale behind these efforts to erase our history is that a focus on the harms of slavery and racism makes white people feel bad; some also claim that this line of thinking is an attack on our country. Of course, even a cursory look at history makes it clear that racial stratification and discrimination continue.

Similar discussions are happening in other nations, with countries taking pride in being empires but avoiding conversations about colonialism. It is also worth noting that many people in the US and abroad are aligning with white nationalism and supremacy.

On the other hand, in the last decade we have also seen a sharpening of a focus on race and racism. This has included a deeper exploration of anti-Black racism globally, as well as efforts to engage the concept of structural racism and not just individual bias. This is important work.

Let's also consider whether a *danger* actually exists that focusing on othering will detract from addressing race. One might offer, as Omi and Winant did, that racism, properly understood, continues to be the dominant form of othering in the US. If that is true, then why would I not choose to focus exclusively on race rather than expanding the discussion to othering?

More importantly, what will allow us not only to *articulate* a useful frame but to move beyond the marginalization created by race, racism, segregation, and separation?

Othering properly understood would *deepen* our understanding of race and racism but would not do so at the expense of understanding other expressions of othering.

Racism is an expression of othering. Othering is the general and racism is a specific, but it's not the only specific. (I write more about this in *Belonging Without Othering*.) In fact, the more deeply we grasp othering, the more it will sharpen our understanding of racism—while also making space to address additional expressions of othering through widening our understanding of how these dynamics work together.

Othering does not call for us to deny race, and yet focusing *solely* on race may keep us from seeing some of the deep structures and patterns of othering. Such an exclusive focus may also cause us to ignore othering that is not race specific. I was recently at an event in Belfast, Northern Ireland. One of the speakers shared that when she had spoken about groups being othered, she was challenged because she was a white woman. How would she be one to know and speak with authority on this issue? She replied to her critics that many people who are white were nonetheless being othered, and were othering, during the time known as the Troubles in Northern Ireland. This othering was based on religion and was responsible for enormous violence. My point here is that even if this woman is white, I do not believe she should be disqualified from speaking on issues of race or of othering. Othering does not prevent us from discussing anti-Black racism, but sometimes the way we think of anti-Black racism may obscure or diminish other expressions of othering.

Othering describes a generalized process. The content is empty until we fill it in and give it meaning. And yet, just like the inadequacy of asserting that the underlying claim of the other is not real, simply noting the natural emptiness of categories does not take us very far. Our tendency to categorize, and then to ascribe meaning to these categories, seems to be hardwired in humans and other mammals. But the content, meaning, and strength of othering categories are fluid and social, and indeed require work and structures to remain durable.

The debates around whether race is the master form of othering in the US may be somewhat limiting. We are not concerned with the history or conditions in the US alone. And modern-day racism is only a few hundred years old, while othering appears to be older than human society.

Sociologist Douglas Massey notes that othering appears to be a central dynamic of hunter-gatherer societies, while Stanford neurobiologist Robert Sapolsky has gone further in his work, finding some dynamics of othering in primates and other animals. Feminist scholars and authors such as Sarah Lacy and Abigail Anderson challenge some of the assumptions about gender roles in hunter-gatherer societies.

Still, we should be cautious about making deterministic claims. There are examples, scientific and otherwise, that point in a very different direction. For example, in *The Dawn of Everything*, authors David Graeber and David Wengrow explore archaeological records to posit new understandings of early societal formations as collaborative and open to cooperation with other groups. Their work complicates the popular understanding of hunter-gatherer societies, including theories about their small size as well as how they organized themselves in groups to defend against others.

More expansively, to simply assert that racism is the dominant force in the US might cause us to miss that othering is a global phenomenon both now and throughout modern history, even before race became salient. We need to see how othering is showing up all over the world, including how it works in concert with racism. If we move beyond the exclusive focus on race as we think about othering, we can open up the possibilities for how we address othering and racism in different contexts and times.

When we move beyond modern history, we find numerous examples of belonging and equality that many today may have trouble imagining. In his work on the long arc of equality, Darrin McMahon asserts that humans have a lengthy history of hierarchy and violent othering, as well as an even longer history of relative equality and belonging. He provides his answer to the question of whether we are wired for cooperation and equality or inequality and domination. His answer is: both—and therefore neither. There are simply too many contingencies to permit a single clear response.

So, while I use many examples of racism as a primary site of othering, a focus on race is not the core realm of this book. Instead, I join the very real issue of race with the frame of othering to illuminate not only race in new ways but other areas of inequality as well.

A similar question arises about those other areas of inequality: Why use othering rather than naming other forms of marginalization, such as religion, gender, or disability? All of these categories, and more, have indeed been used to define groups as other. And while each is different in its expression, the processes of creating marginality share a similar structure. But, while focusing on the specifics of various expressions of othering might be necessary to promote belonging, it will never be sufficient.

As a researcher, I found that othering went furthest toward illustrating the way these forces work globally and historically, phenomena that are not explained by using only a frame of, say, racism or religious persecution.

Othering speaks to the many different expressions of bias that we see in society. But again, we must be careful not to simply move to neutralize bias or reduce it to the unit of the individual. Othering provides a framework that reveals processes that spread inequality and marginalization. Othering is expressed through the refusal to fully recognize one another. Othering happens when we segregate ourselves from one another. Othering occurs through hoarding of opportunity and denial of full participation in society.

And, importantly, othering works through the act of denialism itself—the refusal to acknowledge others' stories or histories, perhaps even others' place in a shared future.

Othering can help give shape to many variations of prejudice when the existing categories don't quite work. It's not uncommon, for example, to hear reporters refer to Islamophobia or ethnocentrism as "racism," although religion and ethnicity are not racial categories.

The fact that so many leaders and writers today fumble when describing expressions of bias and prejudice underscores the lack of an accessible frame that reflects the full set of intended meanings.

Othering is the process of denying an individual or group full respect and dignity that would accord them all the rights and claims we enjoy. In its assumption and practices, othering considers the other as less than—less desirable and often less grievable.

The entrenched othering of groups does not happen primarily at an individual level. Enslaving Black people required the full weight of the government, the military, religious institutions, and culture in collusion with the larger society.

Othering at a group level requires social structures and stories to become durable. Even when social dynamics are clearly structural, we are likely to see them through the lens of individual practices. This is especially true when considering unfavored groups. The fact that Black Americans as a group have less wealth is more likely to be explained by the lack of individual drive than by the structural arrangement of wealth creation, such as home ownership, which is driven by racialized lending practices.

Othering is a broadly inclusive term but is a sharp enough word to point toward a set of common dynamics, suggesting something fundamental about how we experience and embed exclusion within our societies. The mechanics of othering can be independent of any particular group.

Let's get deeper into those mechanics now.

Reflect

- Where have you noticed narratives of *us versus them* lately?

- Can you think of any examples where you have been in a group and been asked—directly or indirectly—to push others ("them") away in order to safeguard the "us"?

- Are there people or groups who feel *other* to you? What fears or concerns about erasure might be present when you think about the other?

- We may never be able to understand what someone else has experienced, nor can they fully know our experiences, but we know that grief is a shared human emotion we all carry. Have you ever acknowledged someone's grief? What happened next? Does anything change inside of you if you begin to acknowledge that the other carries grief and you have this in common?

3

Is Othering Natural?

Now that I have explored *why* I use the frame of othering in addressing our most seemingly intractable challenges, let me go further into how othering works and some of the consequences of othering.

It is important to note that the effects of othering vary greatly, depending on who is doing it and why. I am concerned with these dynamics primarily at the group level. Interpersonal contexts do not have the power that the state and the law have. State-imposed othering is very different than my break with family that I described in the preface. No one would call the police in my family situation.

While both personal and wider social situations are important, the power and reach of the state are largely unparalleled; therefore, othering cannot be addressed solely at the interpersonal level.

Similar claims could be made about the importance of culture and norms in producing and sustaining othering at a group level.

Of course, one may be othered at the meta or state level *and* at the interpersonal level; in fact, this is often the case. When the US government breaks with China over the coronavirus or trade issues, we should not be surprised that what quickly follows are Americans engaging in personal attacks on people who are assumed to be Chinese. Most of us will not conflate individual Americans with US government policy, and yet we often do this to others; for example, all Palestinians become Hamas or all Jews become the Israeli government.

When the work to understand othering identifies the problem as between two people, this often leads to blaming or trying to change only individuals. But much of our fragmentation today is happening on a group level with an underlying structure—othering—that can easily be employed.

The stories that leaders engage in are about the other are in *that* other group. It is not *I versus you* but *us versus them*. Conflict between two groups has more significance than conflict between two individuals. Put another way, groups are not othered because they are different—they become different because they are othered.

We will continue to use the concept of groups to help us make sense of both othering and belonging.

Is Othering Natural?

There is a long-standing assumption that one will naturally favor one's own group. This is often referred to as *in-group and out-group favoritism*. Significant research shows that we seem to be hardwired to develop categories, including in- and out-group categories.

The Polish social psychologist Henri Tajfel found that groups can be arbitrarily assigned by creating a bias for one's own group and creating a bias against the other group. The bias that distinguishes each group could be of no significance. This powerful research has been replicated many times and has helped to buttress the position that we naturally create groups and then discriminate.

This assumption often leads to people suggesting that the process of othering is inevitable, that it is deeply wired into our brains and dictates our behaviors—in other words, that we are programmed by our evolutionary history to favor our own group. We have been creating groups since our earliest social formations, when we existed in small bands and our survival was dependent on trusting people with whom we had daily and lifelong contact. This historical view has caused many people to think of othering as a type of tribalism that is not only natural but also inevitable.

I believe this is too simplistic and does not fully explain what is happening today.

First, extensive work done around in-group and out-group theory struggles to explain what is happening when a group engages in a negation of *itself*. Dominant groups are less likely to have a negative in-group assessment. The entire society and culture are constantly reasserting the value of the dominant group. Marginalized groups are often trying to measure up to a standard that they did not set. It is not supposed to be that way. Men have historically attempted to dominate women, for example. When this tendency is enshrined into daily practice in larger society and is taught from religious texts, should it be surprising that some women may also accept the assertion that men are better than women? That is a kind of in-group negation.

In works such as *Behave*, which look at ways humans and other animals organize themselves, author and scientist Robert Sapolsky reacts to this phenomenon with one simple word: *weird*. He asserts it is just "weird" we would harm ourselves—our own group—if we are supposed to know, trust, and love ourselves.

This dynamic may make more sense, though, when we understand there are dominant stories to which none of us are immune. The imprint of these stories often takes place largely without our noticing.

What may be more surprising is when people in the dominant group push against dominant stories that would ostensibly benefit them. For example, a man, who not only experiences the same social messages about gender roles as a woman but is the apparent beneficiary of a society where men are viewed as superior, rejects that story. This rejection often goes beyond symbolic implications, as the dominant group is in a position to bestow both material and symbolic benefits.

When I was doing work in an African country years ago, daily life and norms made explicitly clear that males were of higher value and smarter than females. When I was eventually offered a permanent job in this country, I declined. Some of my colleagues were surprised. If I liked the work and the terms seemed good, why would I turn the offer down? One of the main reasons was my concern about how women were treated. But at that time, many of my male and female friends didn't see anything so controversial about the general belief that boys were better than girls, at least certainly not enough to turn down a good job.

I am not pointing to a blind spot of this African country (or my friends) to lift up my own clear vision. Instead, I am suggesting, as Mahzarin Banaji and Anthony Greenwald assert in their book *Blindspot: Hidden Biases of Good People* (on how the mind and particularly the unconscious work), we *all* have blind spots, individually and collectively. I am also suggesting that we are all part of social arrangements that come to be seen as natural and inevitable—what has been labeled by Brazilian philosopher Roberto M. Unger as "false necessities."

And a large part of what I am calling for in this book is a rejection of a story that is based on a false necessity. I shared my concern as an eleven-year-old for Chinese people even though I did not know anyone from China. I did not show the same empathy for the rights of gay people until much later in life. Our stories, meaning, and structural arrangements are largely social and not just given to us by biology or some other force beyond our control. In discussions on sexuality, it is often claimed that there are natural sexual categories and gay and nonbinary people are choosing to violate what is natural and therefore deserve no empathy. I did not fully appreciate the problem with these claims until I was an adult. One of my many blind spots.

These stories are not just about what we believe; they become material facts expressed in the arrangement of everyday life. Reductive stories not only reduce the present but also limit our collective imagination of what *could be* possible as well. It may be more difficult to imagine a female president or pope in a society where they have never existed.

We tend to assume a degree of *naturalness* for whatever *is* now. The naturalness that we assume when we are talking about individuals, we replicate in our assumptions about groups. We too easily assume that people naturally want to be with their own group, with little attention to how a group was constituted and maintained in the first place.

I am suggesting, and will continue to, that there is no *natural* other or them. Does this also suggest there is no *natural* we? Possibly. If there was a *natural* belonging group, we would expect to find it in the family. But even in a tight, loving family there can be deep breaks. As authors Brené Brown and Andrew Solomon demonstrate, families are frequently sites of intense breaking and othering, even as they may also be places of belonging (and even if that belonging is conditional). As we do this work and live our lives, we must remember, we will never be free of all blind spots. The German philosopher Hans-Georg Gadamer reminds us, everything that reveals also conceals. Still, not all othering or belonging is the same. While experiencing the pain of being ostracized in my family, I never worried about physical harm, and I knew they cared and wanted what they thought was best for me.

These messy realities make the claims of in-groups and out-groups organized around an idea of *natural tribes* seem at best naïve; they are also radically incomplete. At a deeper level, this also raises a question about the terminology and beliefs associated with tribalism; consider that in Europe and generally in the West there has been an enduring negative association with Indigenous people and practices. Profound stereotypes are linked to the concept of tribalism from the colonial perspective. (For more on this topic, see the book *Savage Anxieties: The Invention of Western Civilization* by Robert A. Williams Jr.)

There are circumstances that are more likely to produce in-groups and out-groups, but these are full of contingencies that can change and disrupt any perception of naturalness.

James Baldwin noted, "We are all androgynous, not only because we are all born of a woman impregnated by the seed of a man but because each of us, helplessly and forever, contains the other—male in female, female in male, white in black, and black in white. We are a part of each other."

Some folks disagree with this Baldwin quote and find it unsettling. There are those who reject the claim of our inherent mutuality. They may be more likely to embrace the notion that some groups are *naturally* superior to others and therefore have a right to dominate. One might also note that Baldwin's statement leans toward a binary that has to be questioned, if not rejected, as we reject that genders are limited to man and woman or sexual orientation to straight and gay.

If one believes that separation is natural and even inevitable—that some are of less value or even pose a possible threat—then the need to dominate and demean may even be seen as an *appropriate* role of the superior group. This story of domination might then be understood as not just an accurate description of the world but a necessary and justified arrangement.

Certainly, this was the justification many white people used to enforce apartheid in South Africa, where I worked for some time. This story of domination was also the belief of many people in the US to justify the enslavement of other human beings and the need to enforce segregation. It is also still the stated position of many people around the world who embrace racial, ethnic, or religious superiority. Such a worldview can easily support the suffering and exclusion visited on the other.

It may be reasonable, then, to assume this question of naturalness with in- and out-groups could be resolved by instead just focusing on the individual. This is often a reframe used when people are confronted with *us versus them* categories. But this is also a false solution. The individual is no more natural a category than the *us* and *them* groups. Certainly, the story of the freestanding, self-made individual that is deeply embedded in Western society is not only a myth but a dangerous one.

Social science research suggests that we should be careful about taking the position of inevitability. Despite many heavyweight thinkers, from Freud to Hobbes to Hegel, who concluded that we are hardwired to be in *us versus them* groups, subject to the bruteness that this suggests, there is growing evidence that we are also wired to help one another and cooperate. In her book *Seeing Others*, sociologist Michèle Lamont argues that this us-them formulation is simply wrong. This evolutionary determinism is also rejected by Stanford University social scientist Geoffrey Cohen and others. Some studies even suggest that cooperation comes to us faster and more spontaneously than hoarding and competition.

I do not find it particularly *weird* when someone from a marginalized group identifies with the more dominant group. This is especially the case if there are clear benefits extended from the dominant group. What I find of more note is when a member of a more dominant group identifies and sides with the more marginal group. Even if the more marginal group bestows praise on such a person, from a material perspective it would seem the marginal person has little to give. Nonetheless, I do not find this situation *weird*. Why would a man side with a woman when he could apparently benefit from male domination? In part because he is not solely defined by his maleness, whatever that is. As Baldwin suggests, he is also partially defined by her femaleness.

Another way of approaching these questions is to return to my story as an eleven-year-old. Is it *weird* that I would side with Chinese people instead of my family and even God? Of course, it would be more accurate to say I was embracing the diginity of all humans. But that may not sound like an eleven-year-old. Such a decision, if you can even call it that, was not made to gain some clear tangible benefit. It was in part a reflection of who I was. I was siding with my humanity as I understood it.

Geoffrey Cohen redraws this debate about inevitability and human nature by suggesting that our line of inquiry may be off. As he states, "The key question is not 'What is our nature?' but 'What are the elements of situations that draw out the better angels of our nature?'"

I would join Dr. Cohen in this inquiry and add to it. How does the way we are situated—our context, our environment, how we are perceived—impact not just our better angels but all aspects of our lives? I'll return to the importance of *situatedness* later in the book, but it's enough to note now that our contexts are full of constraint, contingency, and possibility all at once. We are never only our situatedness, and we are also never completely free of it, just as the complexity of our being is never solely the sum of a certain set of attributes, but neither are such attributes irrelevant.

And while who I was at eleven certainly was shaped by my being raised a Christian, growing up Black in Detroit, and being a part of my particular family, to stop there would be to miss a larger reality than what these elements reveal. My parents suffered, and much of their suffering stemmed from being racially *othered* in a segregated society. That suffering and *othering* are real and have taken years off the lives of my family members—and have even killed some of them.

But as I know and am attempting to share, the story of my parents, of me, and of my family is always more than the sum of our attributes or our suffering. It is in this nuance and multiplicity that *bridging* can happen, which I'll continue to affirm in this book and in my work.

If we are to advance belonging, we must stop assuming or at least mount a serious challenge to the idea of othering being natural or inevitable. While we may not be able to make sense of the world without categories, there are still a great number of possibilities available to us.

The book *Making All the Difference*, written by my brilliant friend, Martha Minow, suggests that there is no *natural* meaning to difference. One might even say there is no natural difference. Differences are made by the meaning society gives to differences. One of the questions Minow asks is, essentially, "What difference does a difference make?" Colin Powell broached this question when Barack Obama first ran for president. The country seemed obsessed with the question of whether he was Muslim or not. Powell responded with his own question: "What difference does it make?" Knowing well that it both would make a difference and that it should not. As symbolic animals, we are not simply determined by our experiences. We have the need to give them meaning.

But we must also understand that once differences are made and given meaning, it will take real work and examination to change our stories about difference.

Othering to Belong

I want to suggest something else important about the practice of othering that might be counterintuitive. Psychologist Abraham Maslow is credited with developing a "hierarchy of needs" that shows, in order of priority, the basic needs we must have fulfilled as humans to survive and flourish.

In Maslow's hierarchy, belonging is listed as humans' third most important need, with the first two being food and safety. Belonging for Maslow entailed love and connections to others, which included family, friends, loved ones, and social relationships. Later scholars of Maslow's work have reordered the hierarchy and placed the need to belong as the first and most primal need, reasoning that one cannot secure food or safety unless one belongs. Being forced out of one's group could literally expose one to starvation and other life-threatening dangers.

But if Maslow's hierarchy is right and one of our most basic needs *is* to belong, then why are we so quick to other and to engage in breaking?

Part of the answer is that we other in order *to* belong.

A prime example of this is in a retelling of the death of the ancient Greek philosopher Socrates. The common version of the story is that Socrates loved truth so much that when he was arrested by the state and given three choices—to stop teaching the truth, to leave his home in Athens, or to be put to death—he chose death. One interpretation held that for Socrates, there were actually only *two* real choices—to be put to death or to stop teaching the truth. The idea of leaving his group was not a real option, as expulsion and isolation, for Socrates, was a fate worse than death. It also would have been the same as death, because it would have represented a spiritual death, the severance of one from community.

But how does this relate to othering? The answer is straightforward.

A dominant group can be constituted by separating itself from other groups and then othering, including one of its own. Groups impose rules for membership, and a frequent group norm is to exclude the designated other or make an other out of a member.

The anxiety and fear associated with these dynamics have roots in not just the physical survival but also the psychological survival of groups. Engaging in othering is often done in response to an existential threat and an ontological condition. While *existential* and *ontological* are often used interchangeably, I am using them here with distinct meanings. *Existential* is about something existing or not—i.e., "Will our group continue to exist?" While *ontological* refers to the meaning and nature of your group: i.e., "What does it mean to be an American?"

What is clear is that the fears of the dominant group need to be better understood before we can move beyond fragmentation and othering.

Institutional and Interpersonal Othering

We have all experienced the discomfort of being somewhere where we felt we didn't belong, but being othered at the governmental or institutional level has a much more enduring impact. When laws are codified about groups or are applied differently to different groups, othering can have devastating and even deadly outcomes.

Not only are the consequences more significant than interpersonal othering, state-based and institutional othering can remain the most durable and hard to change. The Kerner Commission report stated that Black people knew what whites refused to acknowledge: segregation was done for the benefit of whites, with the state utilizing its power to enforce. In *Brown v. Board of Education*, the Supreme Court stated explicitly that segregation was a message to Black students that they were less than, a message that the court indicated these students might never recover from.

This type of othering is structural, and it is also a story that becomes part of our national fabric. This type of othering makes it easier to lock people up or separate children from their parents. It allows us to create hierarchies of who belongs, who deserves consideration and respect within our societies, and who is denied these things. This story insists that certain people, lives, and deaths are more grievable than others. (For more on this issue, see Judith Butler's book *The Force of Nonviolence*. I understand Butler to be asserting that the other is not grievable.)

The call for Black Lives Matter, which gained national prominence following the police killing of unarmed Black teenager Michael Brown in Ferguson, Missouri (and global prominence after the police killing of unarmed Black man George Floyd), comes into very sharp focus against the visible proof that Black lives appear to *not* matter. When we look at the underlying concern that Black Lives Matter came out of, it was not just about one singular case of a Black person dying at the hands of the police or others. And the movement was not interested only in stopping police violence, such as in the killings of Floyd, Breonna Taylor, Philando Castile, Freddie Gray, and Alton Sterling. Black Lives Matter was also speaking to fears that the police would be exonerated by the criminal justice system. And exonerated again by the general public. And exonerated again by the media. And again by lawmakers. And so on. Black Lives Matter revealed the concern about so much more than just the relationship between Black people and the police: it articulated relationships between Black people and all parts of society and made that connection global.

In a public conversation I had with the exiled Turkish author and journalist Ece Temelkuran, she noted that in her work interviewing struggling Turkish families, while the sting of poverty was real, that paled in comparison to the sting of being treated as *not mattering*—not being seen by society, not being viewed as having dignity. Or, in the language of this book, the sting of being other.

Many expressions exist of othering and breaking, on one hand, and of bridging and belonging, on the other. There is the other who is ever present in our stories and our imagination. They are the other deeply feared or resented. There is the other who is constantly presented as a threat, a deviant, or worse. This is the explicit other. But there is another other: the other who is *not* in our stories or imagination. The other who is all but invisible. Many Indigenous people and people with disabilities have too often fallen into this category. We who are non-Indigenous or non-disabled simply don't think of them. Or if we do, we place them in an imagined past.

The othering dynamic is a process that is constantly interacting with our environment and the meaning that comes from our changing stories. While our evolutionary history and our need to belong are important to understand, we must avoid a simplistic, deterministic story of othering and breaking. There are things we can and should do to help shift us away from constant breaking and othering. One of those things is to engage in more complex stories about ourselves and the apparent other.

We might also note how much work it takes to keep a group in a permanent place of not belonging. As we will see in the next chapter, much of breaking and othering is motivated by the desire and need to belong.

Reflect

- Have you ever become aware of a personal blind spot? How did you find out you had this blind spot? What did you do?

- Have you observed a blind spot in someone else? How did you recognize it?

- What aspects of your identity align with dominant groups in society? What aspects of your identity align with marginalized groups in society?

- What examples of state or institutional othering have you observed or experienced?

- Who is the explicit other in your stories?

- Who is the invisible other?

- As you continue through the book, consider: How might you bridge with each of these groups?

4

Breaking and Othering

We all know the expression that "seeing is believing." But there are reasons to turn this expression on its head and instead assert that *believing is seeing.*

What do I mean by this, and how is it useful in bridging?

I am suggesting that how we see the world is greatly impacted by what we *expect* to see. A simple example might occur in a sports match when a referee calls a foul on a player: our preference for our team is likely to impact our judgment on whether it was a legitimate call and who was to blame.

A more harmful example is demonstrated by the work of American social psychologist Jennifer Eberhardt, a professor at Stanford University. Her research on the association between race and crime has shown that people who were exposed to images of Black faces and were then shown a blurry image were able to identify it as a gun more quickly than those who were exposed to white faces or no faces. These pictures were shown too rapidly for the conscious mind to identify features. The association people made speaks to the association of Black men and guns in our society. Yet this association is not *factually* accurate. White men are in fact more likely to own guns than Black men in the US.

Other examples abound. If a teacher expects students to do well, the students are likely to do well. If the teacher expects students to act up in class, the teacher is more likely to observe the students acting up. This is not just true of teachers but of all of us: *we see what we believe.* So common is this phenomenon that it actually has a name: *confirmation bias.* We see the world in ways that are consistent with our biases or beliefs. While we consider the idea that there is no natural other, which I am claiming, we know that there is still othering. So let's turn to *breaking* to make sense of this seeming paradox.

Making the Other

Let's first consider how the other has been made.

When you read science, law, or popular culture from the nineteenth century, you'll find a plethora of discourse that was based on the idea of an essential, natural difference between races, as well as a natural hierarchy of races. Scientists and others made measurements of body parts, including the skull, to try to explain why races were naturally different.

At the same time, other scientists began to question the very foundation of race itself. Consider the fact that every ten years in the US we have a census where races are categorized and counted. Yet the categories are not stable. Who is considered Black, white, and otherwise in one census may be considered of a different race in another. When I was born, I was called "colored." Later I was considered "Negro," then still later, "Black." These were not just changes of labels but changes of meaning and social status. Recently California and other government entities have tried to figure out who is Black for the purpose of reparations. It turns out this is anything but a simple question.

Breaking is one of the core ways we constitute and maintain an other. Breaking does the heavy lifting of othering. Breaking suggests that we see the other as not just different from the we, and therefore less deserving, but possibly even a threat.

While othering is focused on the very constitution of the in- and outgroups, breaking is more focused on method and practice. Breaking is how othering is accomplished and maintained. Breaking moves us closer to othering, while bridging moves us closer to belonging.

Othering and breaking are closely associated, but they are also distinct. There are many different levels of breaking, with different consequences.

I will use Susan Fiske's stereotype content model to help us make better sense of the group dynamics I think are important to understand with breaking. Along with her colleague Amy Cuddy, Fiske developed this model by looking at what I would call othering and belonging along two axes. One axis is *warmth*, or how much a group is liked. On the second axis, the relative *competence* of each group is ranked. The model has been used to measure how much a society envies, despises, admires, or pities social groups, defining these in terms of how "warm" we feel toward a group and how "competent" we feel a group is.

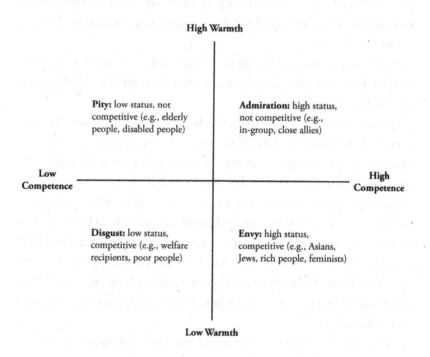

High Warmth

Pity: low status, not competitive (e.g., elderly people, disabled people)

Admiration: high status, not competitive (e.g., in-group, close allies)

Low Competence

High Competence

Disgust: low status, competitive (e.g., welfare recipients, poor people)

Envy: high status, competitive (e.g., Asians, Jews, rich people, feminists)

Low Warmth

Graphic adapted from the stereotype content model, from Fiske et al. (2002), by the Othering & Belonging Institute.

Notice in the stereotype content model graphic that all but the groups who are high in both warmth and competence are to some extent *othered*. But these three groups are quite different, and they are othered in different ways. The group that is low in warmth (low) and high in competence (high) is likely to be envied. In the US, Asian Americans and Jews may often fall in this category. On some level they are respected, but they are also excluded to a large degree. In the high warmth/low competence group, which is liked but not considered competent, we can expect to find elderly people or people with disabilities. Women often tend to fall in this category as well. The emotional response to groups in this category falls toward pity. Children are also generally thought of with warmth but as not competent, which is why we create laws to protect them but not empower them.

Then there is the group that is considered low competence and low warmth (low/low). Not liked nor considered competent, this group is even liable to be despised.

Fiske's research was empirical. She and her colleagues not only surveyed different populations to assess what feelings people reported about different groups in society, but they also measured brain activity to track how peoples' bodies responded. There is a region of the brain that lights up when we see another human. But when study participants were shown images of people considered to be in the low/low category, in many respondents that part of the brain did not light up. Instead, what lit up was the part associated with disgust, the same area that holds feelings about nonhumans, such as insects. (When one group calls another cockroaches, they may be speaking more than metaphorically.)

The care that we extend to these groups is consistent with their *status*. If the high/high group, or our in-group and close allies, are having difficulties, we are likely to see and tell stories of *a system and society* that is not working for them. If a group is low/low and having challenges, however, we are more likely to see and tell stories about *the group* and its members failing and being undeserving.

When former President Ronald Reagan asked us to reserve our empathy only for "the *deserving* poor" (my emphasis), most people understood implicitly which group he was referring to as deserving and which group was not. This distinction fell clearly around racial but also gender lines.

It is not so much that we believe what we see as that we see what we believe. In more of Eberhardt's work, experiments have shown that when respondents subliminally see a face of a Black man, they are primed to see a gun. This expectation is not limited to whites; Blacks also expected to see a gun faster after having subliminally seen a Black male face. Seeing a face at a subliminal speed means the conscious mind has not even registered the face. But white people may have a stronger expectation of a gun than Black people. (For more on these findings, see Eberhardt's book *Bias.*)

It is important to consider this more deeply. Why is there a persistent stereotype about guns and Black men? Does it mean white people or maybe all of us are racist against Black men? What does information like this do to the claim of being "colorblind" or of being able to go "beyond seeing race"? What about the aforementioned fact that white men are statistically more likely to own a gun than any other demographic group in the United States?

Let's fold this into our discussion of *othering* and *breaking*. First, I would like to clear up a few things. Stereotypes are often not factually accurate—but neither can you weaken the strength of a stereotype with facts alone. Second, stereotypes are generally not individual or personal. The impression of Black men with guns is part of our *social* story. If the story is widespread, it is likely to have an impact on all of us, including Black people and those who would like to think they are colorblind.

Having these stereotypes doesn't necessarily make us racist, but it can have real life-and-death consequences that are deeply racialized. The unconscious is not interested in being colorblind. When a police officer claims that a Black person had a gun, erroneously or not, they may be honestly reporting what they thought they saw and still be wrong.

They may be a white police officer or a Black police officer. Many statutes exonerate a police officer who kills someone because they claim they feared for their own life. This may sound more reasonable when we realize that an underlying story in America has been that one must be afraid of Black people; that story is played out across many areas of American life. The perception of a racial other creates a shared collective experience. If Blackness is seen as a threat, the very idea of Black innocence is called into question in the national story of the United States. So that even Black children, like Trayvon Martin (seventeen when he was killed) and Tamir Rice (aged twelve), are seen as a threat. They are seen as older than their years in a way that makes them less sympathetic and deserving. Again, it matters little to the unconscious that the story of Blackness being a threat is factually inaccurate. Notice that when these stories are widespread, they not only impact the dominant group but are likely to impact how members of the "despised" group see themselves as well.

As the Fiske model shows, there are different degrees of othering and breaking. Elderly folks may be othered, but they're still seen as human. When it comes to the citizens of the most disparaged quadrant (low warmth/low competence), however, it has been shown that many people, at an unconscious level, don't see people in this group as fully human. As I said, this has dangerous and even deadly consequences.

Earlier I discussed how many men, and even some women, consider women lesser than men in several regards. But in this story women are not necessarily seen as a threat (even if the biblical story of Adam and Eve might suggest otherwise). In the Fiske model, the woman may be liked and even loved, but not respected. She may be pitied and not accorded the full rights of all members of the group, but she is a recognized member, nonetheless. She may be seen as needing protection from or by the man. Fiske's research is quite powerful. It would be useful to apply it to additional categories of others, including the trans and nonbinary population, as well as newly emerging racial and ethnic categories.

This longstanding story about women was a primary justification for denying women the right to vote and limiting their ability to hold property until the early twentieth century. In this story, women were limited to a set of roles, such as taking care of children and the family, ostensibly for her own good and the good of the larger group. One might also notice that the role of the woman also has meaningful implications for the role of the man.

And consider that the major threat to the life of a woman based on her gender is not the racial, ethnic, and religious other, but the man from her own in-group. That becomes a more complicated story. What are the implications not only for women but for a society that promotes that men are superior and even that the highest divine being is a male god? As a man, I am not necessarily comfortable with the notion of God being known primarily as a man. I have two daughters—can't they be in the likeness of God?

In the church I grew up in, the doctrine was that in a heterosexual family—indeed, there was no other kind recognized—the man is the head of the family, mirroring the belief that God the father is head of the universal family. In my family, these sacred norms were stated clearly, and we were supposed to live by them. The supposed naturalness of these roles was accepted, even if, depending on the family, it was sometimes accepted with a nod and a wink. But the reality was more complicated. We all knew that in many ways my mother was the head of the family, and my dad was, by his disposition, more comfortable in what was then considered a woman's place. Still, social roles impacted how my parents showed up.

This complicated, messy dance occurred in a number of ways in my life. In my last year of high school, I was accepted to Harvard with a scholarship. But I decided not to go. The main reason I decided against going was that Harvard did not accept women. While I knew about Radcliffe as the all-female sibling school of Harvard, the reality remained that Harvard was the school with mythic status and Harvard remained all-male. My family did not know much about formal education, but they did know that Harvard was at the top of the game. They resolutely did not support my decision not to go to Harvard. My mother and my five sisters were confused by my decision. What did the school not accepting women have to do with me? *Weird.* When I tried to explain my reasoning from the perspective of a seventeen-year-old, it did not make sense. I did not then have the vocabulary to speak about patriarchy.

As a last-ditch effort to persuade me, my parents told me that if I did not go to Harvard, I should not expect any financial help, although this was largely a hollow threat, as my family had limited economic means.

I ended up heading west and going to Stanford.

I recount this story to give context to how the wider frames of othering and belonging help us make sense of the fluidity and messiness of groups, as well as how these frames differ from the narrower focuses of bridging and breaking. My parents in this instance were not saying I did not belong to the family; it wasn't a case of me not following in their footsteps. What they were doing was borrowing the *national story* of what men should do. And in that story, the best and brightest are men, just like God, and the best and brightest go to Harvard.

Why am I rejecting the story of the supreme man? It is not just because I have daughters or sisters or a mother. There is no way my mother should be considered less than my father or obedient to him, nor any woman to any man, nor any person to any other. I don't accept that any humans are at the top of the life chain.

Our identities are complex, and they are also constituted *in relationship* with others. In her book *Sacred Nature*, religious scholar Karen Armstrong posits that as we humans reclaim our connectedness with nature, of which we are a part, then the question of hierarchy stops making sense.

Earlier I challenged the idea of naturalness in the formation of groups. We should be considerate of how the story we inhabit can make it easier or more difficult to free ourselves from the artificial constraints of what is natural to or about a group. These constraints are held together by laws, norms, practices, and stories, and imagination plays an oversized role. If we reject the notion that there are natural groups, perhaps we should then not be so surprised when someone society assigns to one group rejects that assignment or accepts it with their own contingency. Are Black people bird watchers? As the story of Christian Cooper—a Black birdwatcher in Central Park confronted by a white woman who called the police on him for him asking her to leash her dog—shows, at least one is. The social constraints we put on each other will often not fit all of us all of the time.

As I mentioned earlier, evolutionary theory about how, in small tribes, we learned to trust only those in our tribe has been used to explain othering as a natural evolutionary process, the idea being that we're hardwired to have a small in-group and a large out-group. As we have been discussing, this idea is limited on several grounds.

Recent anthropological research shows counterevidence that categories were not necessarily small or categorical. (Again I recommend Graeber and Wengrow's *The Dawn of Everything* if you wish to explore these ideas more fully.) If that is indeed the case, it calls into question the utility of using previous assumptions: if the theory of small tribes isn't accurate, we can't assume that it's natural for us to break into small groups based on category. Moreover, even if our classical view of tribes was accurate for a time, it is not clear how that would explain why today billions of people who don't know each other, such as billions of Christians across the globe, would identify themselves as a tribe in the way that term is being used now. Third, if othering is just a function of our innate nature playing out, why is it more pronounced at this moment in history than in the past?

There is also something unsettling about using the concept of tribes to explain negative behavior. Tribes in the US have often been associated with both the Indigenous other and part of a larger narrative of being "uncivilized" and needing to be constrained. It is somewhat ironic that research from "civilized" societies, who all over the world are responsible for so much decimation of Indigenous life, is used to try to explain current patterns of negative behavior in those same countries as "tribalism."

The question of whether the small tribes theory is accurate is not just an issue of possibly getting our evolutionary history wrong. This error, if it is an error, could lead us not only to misunderstand the nature of the problem of othering today but also to adopt the wrong set of interventions. We must inquire what is driving these dynamics beyond only a narrow concept of human nature. Assigning this practice of othering to our inherent nature does not explain why othering and belonging are not distributed relatively consistently across human societies. Exceptions might give us insights into the rules.

One of the dangers of overemphasizing the traditional story of the tribe and its natural formation is it can cut us off from one another and ourselves. Asserting that we are destined to break off from and "naturally" create others invites a fatalism and false necessity. If it is natural for us to hate and kill one another, if it is natural for us to dominate the other, then we find little hope for the future and for humankind and all other expressions of life. That would indeed be a reason to be apathetic and despondent.

But if a significant reason we other is in order to belong, we might find different ways to approach both belonging and othering. This claim would suggest our need to belong is at least as fundamental as our propensity to other. But this inquiry is not available to us if we make the false assumption that othering and breaking are inevitable or are the result of human nature.

I suggest we approach totalizing claims of human nature with some skepticism. Darrin M. McMahon, in his book *Equality: The History of an Elusive Idea*, does just that. He notes that despite our evolutionary pull, something remarkable occurred in human history. As humans developed more sophisticated language, our ancestors became *symbolic animals*: we became capable of making meaning out of symbols.

One of the important aspects of this evolution is that it gave humans the capacity to create and imagine. This development gave us, to paraphrase McMahon, an independence from our biology. What he is suggesting is that the possibilities of meaning making and culture exploded. We could no longer make sense of life, or our nature, simply through genetic means or evolutionary history. Our evolved ability to engage in symbolic meaning is one of the reasons stories are so essential to us. We are the only animals, as far as we know, that make meaning about death, life, and religion.

McMahon further asserts that inequality and domination are modern practices that developed post–hunter-gatherer phase. That it is civilization and farming that have given us many of current practices of hierarchy. Modernity is only twelve thousand years old, while our time as hunter-gatherers was millions of years. Hunter-gathering simply cannot explain our current practices of othering and domination. As he suggests, and I do as well, we should be more attentive in looking at our institutions, symbols, and stories and less at our biology.

So if our current state cannot be explained by evolutionary tribalism, are there other, more plausible explanations? I believe the answer is yes. I will attempt to raise a few.

Rapid Change and Anxiety

If one group dominating the other out-groups is *not* inevitable or hardwired, then why is fracturing both prevalent and increasing today? I touched on these questions earlier, but it is worth returning to them.

Our sense of well-being is largely dependent on a relatively stable environment. But we are undergoing rapid change in several key areas at once, such as climate, technology, demographics, socioeconomic and material inequality, the recent pandemic, and more. This is not meant to be a complete list, and there may be some other areas you think are more important. The point is that when change happens at an increasing acceleration along any axis, it puts humans under stress.

Changes in our physical and social environment are happening so fast right now that our ability to easily adapt can't keep up. If they were occurring at a slower rate, we might be able to adapt. But when changes happen too fast, we are not only stressed but likely to be overwhelmed. This is true not just for humans but for other animals as well.

I was recently talking to a friend who is in his seventies. He was somewhat despondent. The world he grew up in and the world he expected to live in when he reached his current age don't feel available to him now. Family and friends have passed away.

My friend is African American. The house he has lived in for nearly fifty years is in a neighborhood that went from being predominantly comprised of African Americans to one that is now much more racially diverse. This wasn't a bad thing to him necessarily, but it was a different reality from the one in which he had expected to live out his old age. He said that he'd decided to travel for a while around the country, and had been doing so for some months, in essence looking for a place he belongs. He was in part looking for the neighborhood in which he felt belonging forty years ago. But it is not just that the neighborhood has changed—so has he. He is less comfortable in his body. It at times feels strange and even foreign.

My point in sharing this story is that change can also make us a stranger to ourselves. What then should we do?

Remember that meaning making is one of our tools to help us adapt and give our life purpose. We can sustain more anxiety when we have a way to make sense of our lives. While other animals also have to struggle with adapting to a changing environment, we human animals who orient ourselves with symbolism have a special place for meaning and stories.

To *collectively* deal with social and personal stress, we need evolved structures, cultures, stories, and new symbols. We need to evolve who we are. The need to adapt is not just at a physical level but also at an emotional, psychological, and spiritual level.

We are interacting not just with *what is* but with *what is to come*. Our anxiety and stress are not just about the present and the past but also about the future. This gives rise to such questions as: Should we be afraid of artificial intelligence, or is AI a good thing? Is there too much uncertainty about technology and we just don't know?

What about the wildfires, the heat waves, the extreme hurricanes? Are we safe from the next virus, or is it now a deadly fungus that we should be watching out for? Whom do I trust to help me—and us—make meaning of a world that is increasingly changing and not playing by any recognizable rules?

Most importantly, will there be a place for me and my group in this future? This is a version of the Darwinian notion of survival of the fittest or, in the parlance of this book—the *survival of those who belong*.

In this sense, we are not just afraid of dying as individuals; we are more afraid that our group—those we call family, those whom we see as community—will also die. As terrifying as facing one's death might be, it is even more frightening to think your group or species will not survive.

On some level, this second threat is the more profound one. The Proud Boys who marched in Charlottesville, Virginia, in 2017 did not chant, "Jews will not replace *me*," but that *they* "will not replace *us*." The perceived ontological threat to the *us* has been stoked into a powerful fear that both helps define the *other* and gives meaning to the us.

In *hard breaking* (which we'll explore in more detail in the next chapter), fear, threat, and anxiety all play an oversized role in how we treat the other. If we are not clear about the collective threat of widespread fear and anxiety, as well as understanding how to respond to it, then leaders and influencers are more than willing to remind us.

Hard breaking perpetuates isolation, hardens racism, and builds oppressive systems—while driving our politics and institutions toward antidemocratic and inhumane practices. In hard breaking, the circle of human concern is limited to my in-group, however that is defined. I am not concerned about those outside my circle, and I might even be willing to have them suffer for the benefit of my group. Rapid change combined with a breaking story is a breeding ground for fear, and with a little push, this fear can easily become hate.

I suggested that collective anxiety can become easily weaponized, or storified, by being projected onto a threatening other. When we examine this more closely, however, we see it is not an intuitive response. If I am concerned about the economy or climate change or AI, why should the other play a major role?

Consider the COVID-19 pandemic. There was a collective threat. There was then the possibility that we might join together internationally to fight COVID. But the anxiety that we were experiencing with COVID was quickly reframed as fear of the other. This other included not just the country of China but Chinese people anywhere on the globe. We saw attacks on the streets of anyone who was perceived to be Chinese. We also saw the wearing of face masks, which was largely accepted as a reasonable precaution, turned into an attack on scientists and liberals who were ostensibly trying to take away people's freedom.

These dynamics don't just represent our collective society having automatic responses to anxiety. Such responses are generated by leaders who play an anchoring role in impacting how groups and societies process information. Leaders are helping to shape our individual and collective meaning.

We are more comfortable with our fear when we have a specific target for it. It often doesn't matter if it is the wrong target. But anxiety, unlike fear, frequently does not have a particular source or target to fixate on. And not knowing the source of the anxiety adds an additional disquiet. Both individually and socially we tend to hew more quickly to a specific story than to a vague general story. We struggle with not knowing; we want to know.

When we are reacting with anxiety, it is not necessarily because of any specific change, but rather can be due to a cumulative, generalized change. Anxiety can stem from the fact that we often cannot name what is causing our general disquiet. Humans have a particularly difficult time with the unknown and the unnamed. It is not unusual for us to make up a story or to attach to a story that can help explain our anxiety.

When this anxiety is collective, we need a collective story to help us make sense of it. If I were just alone in my story and concerned only about what was going to happen to me, my anxiety would not produce the social breaking and fragmentation we are confronting today.

Another feature of anxiety and fear is loss of control. This is where a strong leader says they can offer security: "I can fix this scary problem you are facing. I am in control of your behavior." The assurance can be comforting, even if it is patently false.

It is helpful to understand that our anxiety and fear are predominantly activated at an unconscious level in our brains. Much of the activation takes place in the amygdala, which is positioned at the back of the brain and shaped like an almond. The amygdala is one of the brain's oldest parts. It is not the area of our brain that deals with facts or deliberate thinking. It is sometimes referred to as the lizard brain, as it is like a reptilian brain.

It's important to note that the unconscious is not acting primarily as an individual processing unit that is analyzing only individual information, but is largely processing social information. The unconscious then is not primarily individually focused but socially focused. Our unconscious mind interacts with our external environment and with meaning-making mechanisms like myths and cultural imprints to create meaning.

While some scientists reject the evolutionary explanation of fear and argue for a socially constructed foundation for fear, there is general agreement on fear's ability to overpower reason and facts. Stories, not facts, are crucial in this process. A good story talks to or moves the lizard brain. It may be easier, at least for now, to believe that other humans are going to harm you than that computers are a danger.

The threat of the *other*, especially the explicit other, shows up all over the world in different garb. The leader who carries these stories may not believe them, but if they can get one group to believe the *other* is to blame, it is easier to build power. The other becomes the foil for harnessing anxiety.

Because the rate of change will continue to increase, we are likely to see more fragmentation and breaking unless we can come up with effective interventions and new stories.

The Role of Status

Two of the ways we make ourselves feel good about our in-group is to degrade the other group or to have a higher status than them in some way. There is no special pride in winning against dogs or ants. But against humans, that is a different story.

A number of experiments show how important it is for us to have higher status than other groups. For example, one group is told they have two options. They can choose to get more material stuff (for example, money or food), but the other group will also get these things. Or the first group is told they can choose to get less stuff and the other group will get nothing. The latter is the generally preferred choice: "I am willing to have less if the other group gets nothing." This is also referred to as the "spiked fence," where one builds a fence that one does not want in order to anger one's neighbor.

This finding does not make sense from a material perspective. Wouldn't the group choose to have more rather than less? But we are not just material beings. We are also symbolic beings, as I've discussed at length already. Status matters symbolically, and status is about competition. We compare our groups to other groups. We not only want our groups to do better, we want the other group to do worse. There is a German term for this: *schadenfreude*.

High-status groups have status and prestige and often have multiple ways of enforcing both. For example, the high-status group can call the state to restore the appropriate belonging space, a possibility that is not generally available to the person with low-competence/low-warmth status (from the Fiske model we used previously).

High status is associated with an exclusionary type of belonging. For example, in high-wealth neighborhoods or schools in those areas, there is often an assumption about who belongs. In Ohio, I lived in an expensive neighborhood. When people who did not have what we may think of as visible indicators of wealth were present in the neighborhood, homeowners were likely to call the police, and these outsiders were likely to be surveilled and questioned. The tragic killing of Trayvon Martin was a story of George Zimmerman believing

Trayvon did not belong in a certain place. Zimmerman felt comfortable calling the police, sharing this belief, and asking for their intervention. Yet even though Trayvon knew he was being followed, he remained on the phone talking with his girlfriend. I have asked my students if they were being followed by an adult in a vehicle while on foot in their own neighborhood—as Trayvon was—whether they would have called the police. Not one Black male student has ever stated they would have called the police for assistance. While it is less likely that someone of low/low status will tell someone of high/high status that they do not belong, even if that did occur, it would have different implications.

One might have noticed that in the political space, the concept of whiteness has become much more salient than it was a few years ago. As the numbers of Americans who indicate their whiteness is important have increased, we are seeing much more expression of white resentment. A 2021 Pew poll shows that 40 percent of Americans believe white people experience discrimination. What is driving these perceptions is a story advanced by right wing influencers that the declining percentage of whites in the US population means that white people are targets of discrimination.

Research on belonging has shown that white people may feel less a sense of belonging in their daily lives than Black people, especially white men. From a material position this finding may be surprising, since white people tend to have more wealth and power in the US than Black people. But it begins to make more sense when one realizes that many middle-class white Americans are anxious about losing not only material means but their *status*. This finding has been shown to be especially true if it relates to losing status to Black Americans. Many researchers noted this phenomenon after the election of President Obama. Phrases like "they are taking over" and about the Obamas being "uppity" were in wide circulation.

These findings point to status anxiety.

And this is not happening only in the United States. In relation to real and imagined others, foreign influencers and leaders have been more and more willing to stoke status anxiety to promote othering and breaking.

The theme of the new emerging story is already visible. We are no longer awash in stories about the natural superiority of one race over the other. We have at least begun to live like it is not "the natural order" for women to be dominated. We have at least begun the process of listening to people whom we consider different from the historically dominant "we."

A discussion that now garners more of our attention is what *systems and institutions* are better to support human life. I would posit that this is a useful shift, even as it remains too tethered to an existing set of conditions, leaving the possibility for human engagement much too narrow. If a good deal of our behavior is activated by the environment we are in, it may be more effective to focus on the environment than on the behavior. Still, this conversation is no longer seduced by the assertion that our current form of capitalism must continue and is somehow natural. These days the US economy is more likely to be discussed as one economy among many alternate possibilities, instead of as the terminal point to history.

While these are important openings, they are not necessarily all that is needed for the shared, thriving future I believe most of us want to create. Change by itself is radically agnostic and contingent. Change by itself is silent on the *direction* we are promoting. Both Donald Trump and Barack Obama ran on a platform for change, but it's safe to say the types of change they were referring to point in very different directions.

So what is the alternative? I believe we all must engage with and build public and shared space. We must help develop and multiply the spaces where all of us are not just observed but fully seen. We must cocreate our own neighborhoods, yes, but also the world. Our neighborhood *is* the world. Without the trappings of an empire, we must claim the right for ourselves and others to belong everywhere. We can move to create a world where fewer and fewer people belong and have dignity or a world where all people belong and have dignity.

Belonging must be a birthright for all and a global norm to which we can orient our world-building.

Reflect

- What examples of breaking have you witnessed in your personal life? What examples of breaking have you observed on an organizational or institutional level?

- Do you feel that the life you expected to lead is available to you now? Why or why not?

- What social issues give you anxiety? Can you imagine how widespread belonging might shift those issues or that anxiety?

5

Hard and Soft Breaking

There are many different ways to break and many ways to bridge. As the Susan Fiske stereotype model that I shared earlier shows, breaking or bridging toward different groups can happen in very different ways. In the family story I shared at the beginning of the book, there was certainly breaking, but it was always tempered with love and bridging. In this chapter we will consider some of the ways breaking and bridging happen.

Soft Breaking

One possible solution to othering that I have often seen suggested is what I call *soft breaking*. While this might be better than hard breaking and arguably might include some elements of bridging, it is breaking nonetheless.

Soft breaking often shows up in interpersonal contexts. Soft breaking may mean not being willing to listen to someone or not allowing them to fully participate while still accepting them as part of the us or we. When we think back to the Fiske model, recall the groups who are considered likable but incompetent, such as children and older adults. When we don't trust a family member's competency, we are inclined to limit their participation. They are often not allowed to cocreate their own daily lives. For example, a recurring motif about children taking care of their older parents is one of infantilizing their parents, controlling when they can eat or go to the bathroom. There may be a reason to restrict the older parent if they are incapacitated or a danger in some way to themselves or the world. But studies have often shown the control of an older relative goes beyond what's reasonable and can unnecessarily compromise their dignity. Still, there is often love and care and, as Fiske's work suggests, pity. With these types of durable stories—such as the older person needing to be controlled or young children not deserving a voice—it's easier to see how soft breaking looks in practice. It also reminds us again that bridging and breaking are not simple binaries.

Think of soft breaking where someone is diminished but still part of the group. Their belonging is in some sense still present, but it is conditional. Women for millennia have been limited in financial matters by men. They would be "allowed" a certain amount of money (an allowance) by their supposedly more capable husband, father, brother, or other male figure. (Some of us may recall a very popular TV show in the 1950s called *Father Knows Best*.) In these examples, there may even be love or care present between men and women, and women are not entirely excluded. Yet the practice of soft breaking is still predicated on one party or group being less than, not fully belonging, and not having agency to cocreate their conditions.

Inclusion, where someone is allowed into a space or organization but only on terms not set by them, is another form of soft breaking. The terms of engagement are often determined by the dominant group. Even when this is apparently benign, hierarchy and breaking still exist.

The position of *ally* can be another expression of soft breaking. It may be suggested that friendly others, called *allies*, are outside our group and that, at best, they are junior partners, whose concerns are not the main concern of the group.

There has been a lot written on allyship. One example is the call for white people to become allies to people of color in movements for racial justice. Many white people have been more than willing to be allies and become relatively silent partners. In this arrangement, it is assumed that since whites generally have had or still have more power, one of the ways to address that power imbalance is for whites to become allies. The ally role usually has a set of conditions attached, including not speaking unless specifically asked to by the people of color in the group, a strategy where allies step back and let marginalized groups come forward. The logic of this dynamic may come from the fact that, historically, white people were often the only voice at all, and from a social norm that white people speak and engage with more authority. (In the community I grew up in, we would say white people's "ice was colder.")

Strategies on how to engage allies may reflect the need to reset power. As I have discussed, there can be a serious lack of symmetry between more powerful groups and more marginalized ones. This does not suggest that the more marginal group is *without* power, but it does imply that there is likely an imbalance, one that often has implications for breaking and bridging.

Soft breaking undermines and destabilizes true belonging. While it might not be as extreme as complete exclusion, soft breaking still creates an *other*. The story with allies, for example, is they are conditional partners whose role is limited within specific parameters. The role that allies are assigned is not really part of the central *we*.

There is indeed a need for marginalized groups to have the space and the resources to speak and for their vote to carry the proper authority. But making sure the story of a marginalized group is heard should not be predicated on another group being silenced. Because of history and power dynamics, we may have to make some interventions to create spaces and generate conversations that attend to the power differential between people or groups. But any such interventions should be approached with caution, and we must be very clear about intentions. We are not trying to create a world where white people or any people are dominated, but a world where there is *no* domination. And we all have a role to play in building that world.

The concerns, suffering, and aspirations of all groups can and should be placed on the table. This does not mean that all concerns will prevail. But it does mean there needs to be a space for them to be seen and considered.

Soft breaking is where the other is recognized as part of the group but in a diminished capacity. Let me give an example. I was teaching a class at a large university where there were over a hundred students, about half of whom were women. During our class discussions, I noticed that the women were reluctant to speak. And when they did speak, many of the men would make demeaning comments or exhibit disapproving body language. I decided to designate one day a week when only the women could speak during our discussion. Many of the men were very unhappy about this arrangement. After about four or five weeks, I opened the class up so that all students could speak on all days. The women had found their voice and were no longer intimidated by the men, and the class discussion more accurately reflected the balance of the group, as well as mutual respect. Without this kind of true cocreation with others, bridging will continue to elude us.

Although soft breaking still maintains some relationship between people and groups, I have often witnessed soft breaking that is not benign and can be too easily taken up as a strategy, especially in service to practicing inclusion. Remember, our intentions are that we are aiming for a world where none are othered. This is not just an effort between an allied group and a marginalized group, but an effort for a larger society. That does not mean there will be no efforts to make power adjustments to ensure all are heard. But at best this should be a temporary arrangement approached with great care.

There is almost always some asymmetrical power imbalance between groups. But in many cases, the imbalance is minor and does not need robust intervention. One is not likely to see a complete alignment of one group on one side of any issue and another group completely on the other side. In the US, both during the 1960s civil rights movement and more recently in the Black Lives Matter movement, the call for racial justice was multiracial and global, not just between Black groups and white groups.

There are many reasons our group identities will not completely align along one group line. The issues are complex, as are we. Our concerns are also nuanced and multifaceted. We can care about many things beyond any particular social categories, including our own. We should embrace this positive reality with some humility. For example, I don't know what it is like to personally experience being pregnant or needing an abortion, but even given my lack of personal experience, I want to advocate for women's health and autonomy. And it may not be appropriate to reduce my role to only that of an ally—I might have more to offer. While my lack of experience in this area should give me some pause, it should not completely silence me.

Different ways to break exist, with different consequences, which suggests the need for different interventions. There are breaks that are informed by hate and breaks that are tempered by love. There are breaks that are characterized by absence and invisibility. There are breaks that are very transitory, and there are breaks that can last for decades. As I suggested in the story about the rupture with my family, there can be breaking even in the most intimate, loving space. Although my status changed, I still was part of the family. My mother and father were still my parents, and they still fed me and cared for me when I was ill, even though the way of loving was not straightforward.

Remember that for less pernicious breaks, there might be some care, curiosity, and willingness to engage their story: How do *they* experience life? What are their fears and aspirations? But as breaking hardens or becomes our primary position, we are less likely to be curious and ask questions, because we usually assume we already know the answer about the other, and at some point their concerns are simply seen as not as important as our own. In breaking, the other becomes a reductive stereotype of our fears and imagination. The tropes we use to view the other are both flat and extremely limited.

We also apply this flattening to our own group, but not to such an extreme degree. We often define and think of our in-group as a fixed thing as well. Why is this flattening pernicious? A substantial body of research suggests that holding onto a single story and a single identity increases one's anxiety about change and makes one more susceptible to authoritarian tendencies. In the language of this book, I would say it makes us more inclined to break instead of bridge. A single story often calls on us not only to break with the other but to break with the parts of ourselves that are not included in our single story.

When I became the executive director of a large legal services group, overseeing a few hundred staff members, the organization hiring me requested a compilation of my legal and other writings for their records of confirmation. I complied with the request and sent them many of the law review and other articles I had written. After a month or two, I received a call from one of my law professors, sharing that a number of people had contacted him and the law school to verify *who had actually written* many of the articles where I was listed as the author. My employers, including people of color, assumed I could not be the author of all those writings. The message was: I and other people of color belonged, but not fully. Perhaps we could work there, but we should know our place—and that place was not as the executive director. I was brought into the space, but with conditions and questions about my deservedness and contributions.

Similarly, when gay, lesbian, and bisexual Americans were allowed to be in the military, they were put under the provision that they were not to talk about their sexual orientation and no one would ask. You could join, but only under conditions to make others at ease.

Soft breaking can look a lot like being included, but it is not fully belonging.

Hard Breaking

Unlike soft breaking, hard breaking rejects *any* kind of mutual relationship. Hard breaking is not likely to be tempered by care or love. Hard breaking not only denies the full humanity of the other but often identifies them as a problem or threat.

When breaking occurs, it is not just an action: it is also a story and the meaning captured in that story. In hard breaks, the story is about what is problematic and at times threatening about the other. We see hard breaking associated with authoritarianism and ethnic populism. Hard breaking promotes hatred and disgust of the other, often proposing violence against them.

Examples of hard breaking are walls, borders, apartheid, mass incarceration, deeply dehumanizing speech, and at times violence carried out with impunity. This type of breaking can characterize the other as insects, animals, an invasion, a wave. Ethnic nationalist leaders like Donald Trump in the US and Narendra Modi in India argue that the world is scary, unstable, and in decline because of the other. The other is often spoken for in this arrangement but are not likely to be allowed to speak for themselves.

Hard breaking arises from a perceived fear of group annihilation. Think again of the white supremacist Proud Boys chanting in Charlottesville, Virginia, about being "replaced": the threat does not have to be real or immediate, but the anxiety and fear are likely to be. This is the drumbeat of the far right.

When hard breaking occurs, it is much more possible to pass discriminatory and harmful policies directed at targeted groups.

Let me reiterate a few things.

One is that hard breaking turns an anxiety into a fear about the future. Anxiety, as we have discussed, often does not have a specific source but is more of a generalized disquiet. Fear is more likely to be specific. And this specificity can easily be misplaced. The anxiety about a rapidly changing world may be experienced as a fear that is then turned toward a created other.

Groups that promote hard breaks also often romanticize a mythical past, claiming that we will restore or return to that fantasy era. "The future is scary, so let's reject the future in favor of a past that never really was and certainly never will be." Groups that promote hard breaking fear a future that holds the other making claims of belonging.

The majority is often resentful of the marginalized minority. Powerful leaders support and curate these resentments. To promote their views, they make factually inaccurate statements about nonmaterial concerns. While economic precarity is often cited as the reason for authoritarian populism, the cause and solution cannot be reduced or traced to simple economic or material explanations.

What the aggrieved othering group is calling for is not always clear. Sometimes they are calling for purity. Sometimes they are expressing the group's right to dominate. Sometimes domination is verbally rejected in favor of a type of nationalism. More often than not, the nature of the grievance shifts. Underlying causes are not always clearly articulated.

Breaking in general distances us from others, while hard breaking creates a deep fear of other groups, making it easier to accept false stories of us versus them. Stereotypes and stories we hear can either make us curious about other people or make us fearful. But the false story is false not only about them but also about us. Breaking often calls for a simplicity that flattens both groups, though it does so asymmetrically.

In hard breaks, the out-group is all bad, and the in-group is all good. When the in-group comes up short, the story is one that elicits empathy and concern. If the out-group comes up short, the story often elicits scorn. Consider drug use in the United States. When drugs are in the inner city, the stories are about crime and predators. When drugs are in rural areas, often read as white communities, the stories are about chronic health issues, suffering, and pain.

Another example of in-groups being perceived with sympathy and out-groups being perceived with less care is in how patients of different racial backgrounds are treated in the American health care system. There are countless examples of doctors, particularly doctors who are not Black, underprescribing or withholding pain medicine or treatment for Black patients.

This has happened to me. While living in Ohio, I was returning home late one night when three men jumped out of a van and physically attacked me, kicking and punching me, and eventually, after firing a gun in the air, driving off. Neighbors called the police and emergency medical services. When they arrived and got ahold of the situation, they asked how I felt, and I told them I was dazed and disoriented. The medical workers, who were all white, conversed about whether they should take me in for a medical examination; they decided against it, all agreeing I would be fine. I was not examined.

The next day I went to see my doctor, who was white. I told him that I was still dazed and in pain. He ordered some X-rays but said I should just go home and take it easy for a few days, and I would probably be fine.

A few hours later, when I was at home resting, the phone rang. My doctor told me urgently to come back in. He was practically shouting. He had seen the X-ray results, and I had several broken ribs and other injuries. He yelled that my injuries were serious and likely very painful. He continued with a reprimand: "Why didn't you tell you were in such pain?" "But Doctor," I said, "I did." He was not having it and told me I had not expressed the situation with enough clarity.

I understood that the doctor was upset, and took it out on me, partially because he understood that he had not seen me as a full human being, that he had missed clear signals and clear communication. When an in-group is confronted with shortcomings, it is likely to explain it by looking at structures and the environment. When looking at a shortcoming of an out-group, the story is much more likely to be about failure of the group or person standing in for that group.

These stories of who deserves empathy and understanding are pieces of larger stories about the country itself. One story is of America the country helping to introduce the world to freedom and equality as a democracy filled with opportunity. There is the story of a new Constitution that attempted to limit the rule of royalty and elites with the Bill of Rights. There is the story that anyone can become anything they want with hard work and perseverance.

There exists a different story about America as a country of exploitation. A country that is built on land stolen from its native inhabitants and built by enslaved people who were stolen from their homelands. A story where poverty is seen as personal moral failure. This is a story of a racial dominance and freedom erected on ideas of special destiny and dominance.

One story is about an in-group seeing only good things about itself. The other is about an out-group that can see very few, if any, good parts. It is not just that each of these stories is incomplete in an almost deliberately distorting way, it's that they easily lend themselves to hard breaking practices. They are not just about our past—they point to very different futures.

We can look at research on how families discuss political issues during the holidays as a telling example of the dynamics related to hard breaking. A study in 2018 suggested that following the divisive 2016 US presidential election, many families cut short Thanksgiving plans with their relatives of different political persuasions. The study looked at how politics strained close family ties by measuring the duration of family gatherings. During Thanksgiving in 2016, 39 percent of American families avoided political conversations during the holidays, and dinners attended by opposing parties were thirty to fifty minutes shorter than same-party dinners. In the aggregate, that means American families spent 34 million fewer hours connecting or reflecting with families because of political or partisan differences.

While we might see these breaks as being about issues, they also reveal a more complicated dynamic. Groups are splitting not just over the issues but over a rising general *dislike* and *distrust* of each other. Boundaries are being hardened, and breaking is deepening.

Some experiments have shown that people would switch their position on issues for the sole reason of distancing themselves from another group. In other words, regardless of the issue, one may not support it *only because* the other side supports it.

As I discussed earlier, while there is much that demonstrates favoring what our own group chooses, there is also a phenomenon of preferring a bad outcome for the other group, regardless of the preferences of our own group. In other words, we want the other group to lose out more than we care that our group gets their choice.

So we should not underestimate the potential of outright animus toward the other group as a factor in hard breaking, nor should we overstate the importance of the issues as being reasons for breaks between groups.

Domination Versus Interconnection

Our inescapable connection to one another and the earth is well documented everywhere from spiritual texts to the fields of psychology and political science. While there may not be any singular or ultimate convincing truth, there is enough to create a story of interbeing that is more than a little plausible. Breaking and othering as inevitable processes would not only deny the claim of interconnectedness but rule out the very possibility of it. If one believes that separation is natural and even inevitable—that some are of less value or even a possible threat—then the need to dominate and demean may even be seen as an *appropriate* role of the superior group. This story of domination might then be understood as not just an accurate description of the world but a necessary and justified arrangement.

Certainly, the dominant group retells this story to help justify sub-human treatment of the despised other. This story of domination was also the belief of many Americans to justify enslavement of other human beings and the need to enforce segregation. It is still the stated position of many people around the world who embrace racial, ethnic, or religious superiority. Such a worldview can easily support the suffering and exclusion visited on the other. Maybe we should not be surprised that some Americans who are opposed to statements like "Black Lives Matter" are also now suggesting that slavery may have benefited Black people.

We should remember the concept that people are of unequal value is relatively new. In premodern and Indigenous cultural traditions, it was and is often accepted to a much greater extent that we are inter-connected. Many of the world's oldest religions and cultures claim a degree of connection that is largely missing in Western thought. Meanwhile, Europe and the rest of the Western world constructed stories of our separation. The social theorist Max Weber described this as creating a disenchanted world.

Yet simply asserting that the Buddha or Mahatma Gandhi or Martin Luther King Jr. or others believe in our interconnectedness is not proof that it is so. Perhaps we would be more convinced by modern science, medicine, or psychology. There have been countless experiments to show the importance of belonging for humans and other primates. Is this proof enough? Can anyone prove that we are indeed equal and connected? Recall that Abraham Maslow not only thought we were connected but claimed that belonging is one of our most primal human needs.

If we are constituted through our interrelatedness with others, then it is only *in connection* that the individual properly understood comes alive.

One might ask if we can instead prove the contrary—that is, that we are *not* connected to one another or to the earth. Breaking and othering are deeply embedded in our everyday practices at multiple levels. Is this inevitable? Does this reflect our deepest human nature? I have suggested that there are too many contingencies to allow us make these claims.

But we see counterexamples daily, where our cooperation and care for one another is the norm. Political scientist Robert Putnam, based on extensive research in social capital, asserts that society simply could not hold together without our caring for one another, even as strangers. He calls this *general reciprocity,* which involves doing things for strangers without demanding or expecting an immediate return.

Even if care for one another is the norm, ample evidence exists that we are moving toward greater fragmentation. We have a shared agreement that othering and by extension breaking are happening at an extreme level and that both will increase.

I am not suggesting, however, that the breaking in politics is symmetrical on the left and right. A real lack of symmetry exists between the groups claiming the rights of majority status and groups of marginalized people still fighting to be part of the national and political community. While the far right is calling for white dominance and a rolling back of decades of civil rights gains, people of color are more likely to be calling to build a multiracial democracy.

Compromise isn't the solution for this fragmentation. Not only would compromise be deeply problematic in some areas, but often deep power imbalances exist as well.

In a space where we are arguing not simply what the facts mean but what facts are themselves, there is little that I can say that would change anyone's opinion. The more important point for this book at this juncture is to articulate and insist that bridging is not just about creating false equivalence between groups and then compromising toward the middle. While there may be many areas where compromise *is* important, to merely *assume* that compromise is the right approach is wrong. I do not believe there is room to compromise on genocide or slavery.

Many people are concerned that what some call "identity politics" encourages people to identify with a group and promote breaking, so they imagine that finding a neutral space without identities is the way to bridge. But there is no neutral space. Just as there is no place where we have no social identity. What or who would we be without our gender, age, nationality, religious beliefs, race?

It is accurate to say that we can get stuck on a single identity and assume this identity has some kind of essence. But the correction for this is not to be without attributes. The Indian economist and philosopher Amartya Sen reminds us that when we are threatened or excluded on the basis of a particular feature, that feature will likely become very important. If we want people to step into their fluid multiplicity, we can achieve that not by telling them not to identify, but by removing the threat.

If this is what the frame around identity politics is suggesting, it is wrong. It is not identity that is the problem, it is breaking that is the problem.

But how could there be identification without breaking? I have already touched on a couple of important aspects, one being that we use categories to navigate the world. It is virtually impossible to be a self without *some* form of identification. The problem comes when that identification is reduced to something singular, static, or essential. If people are limited to a singularly defined identity—for instance, if women are not allowed to be lawyers—then it is more than appropriate to organize around this exclusion. Notice in this position there is not the equivalent response to men. Men may not organize around being a man, as being male may not only be important for being a lawyer but is necessary. Maleness is the invisible norm. The failure of men to even notice speaks to the dominant norm. I don't notice male truck drivers as men, they are just truck drivers. But if a woman drives a truck, she becomes labeled as a woman truck driver.

Let me restate this. In a world where women are largely excluded, there may be only a few women truck drivers, and they will be noticed. The men are men truck drivers, but more than that, they are unnoticed truck drivers. The unnoticed group is not free of identity, but their identity is so dominant, it seems natural and so goes unnoticed.

But this fails to explain why some societies have been more violent than others. And why expressions of othering and belonging are not distributed consistently across space or time or place.

This more calibrated observation should call upon us to inquire: What are the conditions and cultures where people are more likely to engage in breaking and othering practices? And under what conditions are they more likely to engage in bridging and belonging expressions?

Even if we cannot get to belonging without othering—and I am not ready to accept that claim—it seems more than obvious that we can have *less* fragmentation. If you believed that we could cut cancer by 90 percent, would you reject such an effort because it is not 100 percent? Are we willing to act in the face of uncertainty not just on the basis of certain knowledge but, rather, on our values instead?

I asserted earlier that *othering is the problem of the twenty-first century*. Before saying more about how to move in another direction, I want to suggest what is *not* the answer. The solution to othering and breaking is not more othering and breaking. As the Reverend Dr. Martin Luther King Jr. reminds us, to pursue an eye for an eye leaves us all blind.

Those who support breaking insist that the legitimate *we* can be safe only if the *other* is constrained and contained, if not eliminated. We may allow for the *other* to be in our midst, but they cannot be in control, and their presence and membership is always conditional and in question.

In this story there is a natural order with a small *we* in control, while the bridging story leans toward an ethos that we flourish in the world by the very nature of our mutuality.

If breaking is falsely insisting that people are categorically different than me, wouldn't the answer be to insist that we are all the same? As attractive and intuitive as this may seem, it is simply false. I cannot solve an apparent problem of our differences by wishing them away. What I call *saming* appears to accept the other because they are just like me. But if my ability to care and love is limited to myself, am I capable of true care and love?

When Martin Luther King Jr. was challenged on the idea of loving all humanity, he responded that one could only love God if he loved all that God reflects. Valarie Kaur, in her work on revolutionary love, insists that the stranger is a friend we are just meeting. In the biblical story of the Good Samaritan, the Samaritan stopped and helped a person who was identified as the enemy of the Samaritan people. When asked the question by fellow passersby, "Aren't you afraid of what might happen to you by stopping to help this stranger?" the Samaritan replied that he was more afraid of what would happen to him if he did not stop to help. It is one thing not to bridge and quite another to break.

These complex issues cannot be addressed on a single registry. We cannot just apply one fix to the mind, the heart, the structure, the culture, and so on. Othering and breaking are addressed by belonging and bridging. We will continue to hold that as our aspiration.

Reflect

- Imagine yourself in a conversation with this book. In this chapter on hard and soft breaking, what conversations did you want to have? What conversations would have been harder to start or more difficult to continue?

- Notice where you may have a desire to pull away from some of the ideas in this chapter. Where do you think breaking might figure into your answers?

- Did the ideas about the inevitability of human nature help address anything you've thought about in terms of breaks in your life?

- Is there any breaking you want to address in groups or relationships you are part of?

- What situations make you feel incapable of showing up without breaking? What hurts and fears keep you imagining that some breaks are too big to bridge?

6

On Belonging

Understandably, one might find all the discussion about the mechanics of *othering* and the different types of *breaking* bleak. But all is not lost. There is a more complex story that is also more hopeful. That story is based on a world built on *belonging*.

Belonging, as I am using it, means having the right to fully participate in and cocreate the world you live in. Belonging means your story is fully seen and valued. Belonging means having the right to make demands on systems and structures. Belonging is being respected as an equal human being with full dignity. That sounds pretty good to most who hear it. But belonging is not just what one gets or what one feels they deserve; it is about how we must show up in relationship to each other. Belonging is not just asking for us to be afforded the dignity and the voice that we all as humans inherently deserve; belonging means we must also respect all others in the same way and afford them their dignity and voice.

In a book I coauthored entitled *Belonging Without Othering*, Stephen Menendian and I describe belonging this way: "Belonging is a complex, multifaceted, and multidimensional concept, and is not readily reducible to a set of simple or prescriptive components. It is also dynamic, meaning that it can exist in one context but disappear in another, or appear and reappear in the same context over time.

Nonetheless, for decades, scholars have sought to define belonging and decode the elements that appear to constitute it."

While we hear a great deal of discussion today about belonging, there is no consensus on what it means. A number of scholars have moved from trying to define belonging to trying to measure the elements of belonging. While I support these efforts, most of them focus on a subjective sense of belonging. I believe an adequate discussion of belonging must also consider the *structural and cultural aspects* of belonging, which I attempt to address in this book.

And while the terms of both othering and belonging may seem unfamiliar, and despite gaining more frequent use, the underlying dynamics that define them regularly show up in our daily lives.

There are some important contours that will give us a sense of why belonging is essential and, more importantly, how we might move more deliberately in the direction of belonging.

While the definition of *belonging* I am using may not only differ from others but continue to evolve, the reality is that psychologists and anthropologists have long underscored the basic human *need* for belonging—our human need to be seen, to be respected, to be recognized.

To belong within a community is fundamental to us. When we don't have belonging relationships, our full self can fail to develop.

One is not a guest in this life, but a full member with agency and the right to participate and cocreate. Belonging considers this position as irrefutable.

The Self-Evidence of Belonging

In the American Declaration of Independence, the drafters penned: "We hold these truths to be self-evident, that all men are created equal, that they are endowed by their Creator with certain unalienable Rights, that among these are Life, Liberty, and the pursuit of Happiness."

Some will question the efficacy of these words given that Thomas Jefferson, one of the main authors of the Declaration, was a slave owner. Even by the document's own terms, the phrase is limited to "men."

Of the fifty-six signatories of the Declaration of Independence, approximately forty-one were slaveholders; all were men. Despite these points of pause, historian Joseph Ellis asserts that these are the most potent and consequential words in American history.

The exact meaning of this sentence has been much debated. It is not my purpose here to join that debate. While the precise meaning may never be settled definitively, the direction of its reach is clear—that the right and status of belonging is self-evident and inalienable. We must give these concepts meaning, and the meaning must be provisional, as others both now and in future times will also be called on to give these concepts meaning. That is what the nature of cocreation in belonging looks like.

This statement also set out a deep norm for our society, a norm we must continue to aspire toward.

Another way to define belonging is that it illustrates the belief that we are deeply connected, as I have already touched on and will continue to discuss. This may seem like a strange claim in a society founded largely on the concept of individuality and separation. Indeed, for some, the idea of being connected to or dependent on someone else is frowned upon or even terrifying.

Claims and counterclaims of our inalienable right to have life and liberty often end up raising questions. People want to know: If this is a foundational concept, should we set out to prove it? How can we know it with certainty?

Yet the drafters of the Declaration of Independence expressed the self-evident truth that all are created equal. No proof was required. And what we are asserting in this book is that all people belong. No proof is required.

The Trajectory of Equality to Belonging

I am asserting that not only are all human lives of equal value, but in many ways, we have taken this as a constituting position as a country, as a people, as a world.

We are moving *toward* belonging, even if unevenly and in a contested way.

Every generation is called upon to redefine and give meaning to our core concepts. Equality stands at the center of this practice. From the US Supreme Court to the classroom, from big cities to rural towns, from North America to South Africa, people have made and continue make different meanings of equality.

When Alicia Garza, Patrisse Cullors, and Opal Tometi, three Black women, came up with the hashtag #BlackLivesMatter in 2013, both in response to the exoneration of the killer of the teenager Trayvon Martin and because of the frequent killing of unarmed Black people, it began to spread across the entire globe. What I noticed was that, even within contentious back-and-forth about the movement from a variety of corners, no one outright rejected the inherent and implied declaration that Black lives were of equal value to other lives. I did not really hear much of an explicit rejoinder—"What do you mean that Black lives matter?" Instead, there was widespread acceptance of the concept that Black Lives did Matter.

And yet the genesis, the very need, of the phrase was due to the continued expression that Black lives did not matter.

The arguments related to any pushback to the phrase, I would argue, were not really about denying that Black lives mattered. The objection seemed to be more on the focus *only* on Black lives—"Don't all lives matter?" was a common rejoinder. Of course, the obvious answer is yes.

In engaging with this discussion, I suggested that the call was trying to convey two things. One, the phrase was calling attention to the fact that Black people's lives did not seem to matter; and two, that statement could also be read as: "Black lives matter, too."

The less obvious answer is that all lives will matter only when Black lives matter. And trans lives. And disabled lives. And all lives.

One might assert that our society currently does *not* believe that all lives matter or that all people are of equal value. You would not get objections from me. But in some ways, the debates around the movement to demonstrate that Black lives do matter misses what this declaration, and others like it, are doing and how important they are. At their core, they are making propositions that are *self-evident*, and yet we don't see that in practice. Declarations like Black Lives Matter are ideas and aspirations—moral and spiritual groundings—that not only direct us but also help us to reclaim what it means to be human.

What does this have to do with belonging? Belonging as I am advocating for in this book helps illustrate the same *self-evident* truths—that all people are of equal value, that all lives matter, and that everyone belongs.

That this point is not only irrefutable but foundational in how we approach living together.

How do these self-evident truths move us toward belonging?

I suggested that each generation needs to reengage with and give life to the concept of equality. Martin Luther King Jr. has said that "the arc of the moral universe is long, but it bends toward justice."

I would suggest two additions. One: *We* are the ones who bend the arc; it does not happen automatically. And, two, forces exist that will always push against us, bending the arc against justice.

I believe that over this long arc toward justice, we have moved through extreme state and religious institutions that have explicitly embraced domination and the debasement of human life. Approximately 250 years ago, *equality* was formally adopted by two countries, France and the nascent United States of America. These events are significant because these nations' births were not despite the lack of equality but precisely because of it. In the foundation of these two republics, not only were a compass and a direction set for where we should go, but also a standard was identified for where we were committed to trying to go.

The work of American philosopher John Rawls posits that when a society adopts equality as a norm, it is not that equality needs to be justified, but instead it is *inequality* that needs to be explained.

Back and forth across thousands of years, cultures have shaped our concept of equality and tried to secure for it a place in our societies.

Many Indigenous cultures have played a significant role in breathing life into the concept of equality. (For more on this topic, see *The Dawn of Everything* by David Graeber and David Wengrow, where the authors discuss the example of the democratic governance of the Wendat and the Five Nations of the Haudenosaunee.)

The ancient Greeks also gave us early ideas about democracy, in which people have the right to participate in organizing their society and the rules and laws that will govern. Democracy was ideally not just rule of the people—self-rule—but also the rule of *equal* people.

The fourth century BC Greek philosopher Aristotle wrote much about equality, noting that there were different kinds of equality. One type was *arithmetic*, which required treating people who share largely the same circumstances the same way; and the other type was *geometric*, which requires treating people differently who are situated differently. He believed that a healthy society needs both.

Yet the US seems to be stuck on the idea that equality is *arithmetic* when it calls for everyone to be treated the same. It is easy to see how this constrained way of thinking of equality still limits our approach to equality and justice.

As discussed earlier, the belief that we all matter and are of equal value is not just a political or philosophical construct; it is also deeply religious and spiritual. One of the core lessons of many religions is that we are all children of God or the divine, and that none matters more than the other.

Variations of this insight have led to more than 140 countries eliminating the death penalty. In discussions about whether the state should be in the business of killing its own, people tend to express their belief that the death penalty is immoral because all life is sacred. It is more than a little ironic that many countries that consider themselves built on religious principles still engage in killing their own. And it is disheartening that even for countries that have come to the position that life matters and therefore should not be taken by the state, this position is not then extended beyond their own borders—as if those outside of one's borders categorically become *other* even to the point of loss of life.

The United Nations Universal Declaration of Human Rights states that all humans have basic rights that are to be respected. I believe this statement, taken up by a global cooperative body, continues this long arc of justice toward belonging.

To recap, I believe that we have been, and continue to be, on a long trajectory toward a norm that *all people belong*. I believe this reverence for life should, and hopefully will, extend beyond human life to embrace other expressions of life, including the earth. I believe this is already happening.

Inclusion 2.0

At times I refer to belonging as "inclusion 2.0." Since *inclusion* is a term that has a lot of currency in how we talk about issues of equity, understanding more about inclusion may also make the concept of belonging more accessible.

Inclusion is largely about bringing someone into an already existing culture, practice, or institution. Think of how immigration works in most countries. The immigrant is welcome as a guest in their new country for many years. They are expected in that time to learn the history, laws, and norms of the host country. After some time and many conditions, including one of sufficient mastery, the immigrant may be allowed to stay, but still provisionally and not forever. If after more time the immigrant performs appropriately and provides evidence of that, they may be granted citizenship or a lesser status. They are in an almost perpetual junior status.

This long and uncertain process to inclusion speaks to a narrative and fear that immigrants, especially if allowed in large numbers, might not fit in or—a more frightening prospect for many people—might change the receiving country's culture and norms.

This process is played out in many settings, including schools, jobs, and neighborhoods. The implied question is whether the newcomer other can be accultured or assimilated into the host institution or society? Can the *other* be made into *us*? If so, maybe they can achieve belonging, but it may remain conditional.

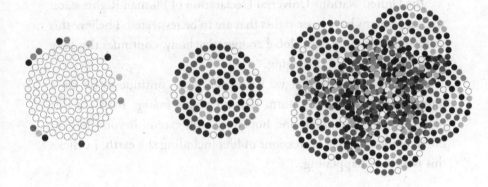

The trajectory of belonging in society, from a small exclusionary "we" toward societies built on the inherent belonging of all. Graphic by Jacob Tompkins and Erfan Moradi; © Othering & Belonging Institute.

Years ago I wrote about the concept of *transformative action*, inspired by trips I took to South Africa and Brazil. Transformative action was in some sense an early prototype for belonging. I asserted that when excluded groups were brought into an institution or setting, it was not appropriate to put the burden on them to fit into an institution smoothly and completely. This is even more the case if the institution was formed with values and norms that are either dominating or hostile to the group being included.

We see this in how protections against hostile workplaces came to be. As more women entered the American workforce in the late 1960s and '70s, they were often confronted with pornographic pictures on the walls, posted by male workers accustomed to an all-male workplace. As women workers began to raise objections to the displayed pornography as inappropriate, demeaning, or just plain unprofessional, management's response often was that since it had always been this way, these women workers would just need to adjust. They could do that by being quiet and ignoring the existing images, or, in an apparent move to equalize, they could put up their own photos alongside the pornographic ones.

The issue eventually made its way to the US Supreme Court, which struck down the right to display pornography in the workplace. Out of the opinion written by the Republican-appointed Chief Justice William Rehnquist, the concept of a *hostile workplace* was born into law.

The reason I share this example—and how it relates to belonging—is that it illustrates the difficulty we have in recognizing that *structures and institutions* are not neutral spaces. Structures and institutions are likely to reflect the values of the majority group who have historically designed them. That reflection of majority values does not need to have any specifically negative intent. In places where groups are historically excluded, the culture and norms are likely to carry messages of exclusion and not belonging. Women were starting to be included in the workplace at that time, but there were clear signals that they did not fully belong. And one might easily imagine that the men who worked in these settings for years would feel resentment about the changes being imposed on them.

But belonging, distinct from just inclusion, carries with it the *right to cocreate* and coconstitute the structures, systems, and cultures we are part of.

Too often a binary arises in how discussions about inclusion take place. Often the old group is concerned that with a new structure being proposed, the belonging and dominance of the original group will be lost in favor of the new group. Even if the new group is let in, there is often an effort to make sure the new group does not disturb the existing norms. And the new group looking to be included may also try to assure the old, dominant group that it will not threaten their existing norms or identity.

To consider the limited nature of this approach, let's look at the effort to racially integrate schools in the United States.

At the height of desegregation in the late 1960s and early '70s, those in favor of keeping students segregated expressed an existential fear that if Black and white children went to school together, they might date, they might fall in love, and some might even marry and have children. In the minds of segregationists, this would pose a potential threat to the existence of the white community, and their resistance was a call to retain purity.

On the other hand, the civil rights groups supporting desegregation did not directly address this concern. Instead, their response was that racial integration was about education, not about dating and certainly not about marriage.

Recall that at that time, a number of states where these challenges were taking place still had laws prohibiting interracial marriage. When the court finally struck down these antimiscegenation laws, it explicitly noted they were built on a foundation of white supremacy, to uphold a notion of white purity. The court ruling against miscegenation laws would change the law but not entirely remove the foundation of those beliefs. Instead, what was set in motion was fear and an insidious backlash. A fear of change and of a new shared future.

So here is the false binary. We have, on one hand, the old group, conservatives who do not want to change. We have, on the other hand, possibly younger or more progressive people who welcome change. This is too often what the discourse around traditional versus progressive is reduced to.

But the issue is not change itself. The issue is the orientation of the change and the impact of the change on our lives and what we care about.

Those who want to hold onto the status quo or return to a mythical past see pending change, often represented by the other, as a threat, sometimes to their very existence. They attempt to keep out the new group or limit the number of its members they allow in. Or if they are let in, they must assimilate into the old group's norms. In response, the new group tries to assure the old group that everything will be as it was. If they do come into the space, they really want the same things as the old group, and there is nothing to fear.

Too often leaders presume they can quiet the old group's fears by telling them, "You might lose something symbolic, but you will gain material benefits." Other leaders who build power by othering may exaggerate the changes that will come and urge resentment and breaking as responses. (For example, in today's discourse the far right has framed immigration as being genocide self-imposed by white people.)

Both positions carry many limitations. For example, having white children go to school with nonwhite children *has*, in fact, increased interracial dating, marriage, and children. In some respect, the segregationists were more right on this than the civil rights advocates. But where the conservatives were wrong was in their proclamation that integration would destroy the white community. Have white communities changed? Yes . . . and maybe. What it meant to be white, Black, or otherwise in the 1940s or 1960s has indeed changed today. Did it destroy or hurt the standing of whiteness? It depends on who you ask.

In a belonging framework, this opposition to having the new *other* join the old *us* speaks to a deep-seated fear that if *they* are allowed to belong, my group will no longer belong. This fear is a response to change. But change is inevitable, and while the segregationists may in some ways be right about change, one could argue that the changes that came about were not the ones they predicted or feared.

Also notice the role of power in this example. One group is allowing another group to join in limited and prescribed ways while still holding onto most of the power.

Belonging without othering will indeed change the nature of groups and communities for all. But a society built on belonging will not entail one group—old or new—dominating the other.

Change will happen in both directions. Both the old and the new group will have some say in the nature and speed of the change, but neither will have everything go their way.

Belonging requires cocreation and coconstruction *among equals*. Belonging is a process of cocreating a new shared future. The cocreation means that the change is not done only at the behest of the old or existing group.

The future *will* bring change. This truth may be uncomfortable. It may be exploited by what journalist and author Amanda Ripley calls "conflict entrepreneurs." But we should not adopt the strategy of falsely reassuring—either ourselves or our communities—that change will not happen.

While we cannot completely control change, we can influence how we adapt to change. Our work—let's call us *bridging entrepreneurs*—then becomes to find ways to talk about change so as to reduce the in-group's fear of being replaced while also articulating that belonging cannot be predicated on another group being subordinate. This is the challenge we must face.

Belonging rejects the idea of domination. No group or person has the right to dominate another. This position should not be controversial. Like the idea of equality, it is already enshrined in many of our norms and documents. The United Nations Universal Declaration of Human Rights begins with Article 1, stating that "all human beings are born free and equal in dignity and rights." One may wonder why, in a world replete with othering, so many countries and people would begin to organize around the position that all people have inherent human rights and dignity.

The Need to Belong

I suggest that much of our othering is being driven by our need and desire to belong, not only to a group but to the future as well. It is the need to belong and the deep fear of not belonging—or of a future where there is not belonging for my group—that is easily manipulated into othering. (This position is brilliantly laid out in the book *In the Name of Identity: Violence and the Need to Belong* by Amin Maalouf.)

Despite the importance of the work of the United Nations and other efforts to bring about justice on a global scale, belonging cannot simply be mandated by law. We can look at belonging at the personal level as well as at the group level. Consider some colloquial statements, like "I don't feel comfortable in this place." The place could be a physical place, environment, or social setting. "I feel like I was born at the wrong time." "I don't belong to this era." "We don't belong here." Consider the message that has come from the trans community, and that many others have also experienced: "I don't feel like I belong in this body." These expressions of not belonging desire attention and help give insight into the myriad ways people belong or not. Even though these may be individual expressions, they represent something much deeper and more profound.

Let's explore what is significant about the subjective nature of these statements.

First of all, our *environment* matters for belonging. Often people experience a sense of not belonging that cannot be easily named but is immediately understood. In the church where I went when I was young, we often sang songs about "going up" (meaning to heaven). Many of the lyrics were about the burden of this life and the possibility of one day going home. These songs carried multiple meanings. Going home entailed dying. Many of these songs had a pathos to them that did not need further elaboration.

Reflecting on these now, I recall that the lyrics of these songs led me to wonder: *What is so disquieting about this life that we yearn, with some ambivalence, to die and go home?* Many believe our fear of death drives much of our lives. We try to keep death at bay. Virtually every major religion weighs in on death and often tries to quiet this anxiety by discussing life after death as a place where we will belong and have peace.

Home is one of the metaphors frequently used to suggest belonging. Home is the place where in theory you are supported and loved. It is the place where you are known and people get you. This is in part captured by the saying "A house is not a home." The desire for a belonging home is universal. As I shared earlier, I, like many, did not easily find home a place of belonging. As I experienced the early rupture with my family and was pushed out of the womb of my psychic and social home, I suffered a deep despair. When the rupture first took place, I remember, as a believer in a caring and loving God, standing on my back porch looking up at the stars with tears running down my face. I stated out loud to God that I no longer wanted to be here. I did not belong. I wanted to go home. An answer came back from my plea. The response was that I could go home when I had finished my work. This response started me on a journey that in many ways I am still on.

In her haunting, beautiful voice, my mother would often sing a hymn that went something like: "In a few more days my work will be done, / In a few more days my race will be won. / Then we can go home where we belong."

The Brazilian philosopher Roberto Unger writes that we are all born into the world homeless, and we spend much of our life trying to turn this life into home.

Some may be more fortunate in that they experience places of belonging. If they do not have a permanent home, there may be places to rest along the way where they are seen and respected. But even those who have a temporary experience of home may feel the constant threat that it will slip away. There are continual reminders that our quiet is indeed temporary. And that suffering and death are never far.

Moreover, if we suffer and have disquiet in our home, we don't have to add to that disquiet. Life comes with suffering, but surplus suffering is a social disease.

Can we put the sting of fear and anxiety to rest forever so that we might avoid the disquiet? I don't think so. As I noted, the disquiet in life is deeply rooted in our being; it may be part of our ontological condition that comes with our consciousness of death and the impermanency of self. And even if we reject this spiritual perspective, we are still confronted with death and disappointment. We may still feel homeless as we journey through life.

Cocreation by All, for All

We may conclude that the group whose identity is predicated on the domination of other groups does not have a place in a world where all belong. I would say there *is* a place for such a group, but with a new identity. I would go further and say that such a world may call on all of us to help create those new identities. We are called on not to control the world, but to participate with others in the cocreation of a greater story. The story may bring in ancient wisdom along with new ways of being. The story will not necessarily be new but will be newly made. And remade.

We can only truly belong to a place when we participate in its cocreation and, in doing so, cocreate our selves into full being. Participation is not control. We have agency when we participate, but not control. Until then, we can practice bridging to that new place. To cocreate requires a different relationship with one another and a different relationship with the earth. Yes, we are also to participate with the earth in this cocreation. You may ask me how. What I would suggest is this: in the same way that, if you want to cocreate with another person, you must be willing to be curious and to listen to them at many different levels, so too must you be willing to become curious toward the earth. We ask the earth our questions, and we listen for answers.

I continue to take solace in the work of James Baldwin. Baldwin did not have many places he felt he belonged. Yet he continually reminds us that we must be careful not to allow the experience of being *other* and the pain that comes with that to be the sole things that define us. Baldwin turned much of his suffering into lessons that he passed down to those willing to receive them. He shows us how to embrace belonging and caring even in a world that tries to deny our belonging. Even if our belonging is limited and we are degraded by members of our fellow species, hopefully someplace and at some time we feel like we belong.

We are concerned not just with our own belonging but also that of our group—and not just now but in the past and, importantly, in the future. Can we belong when much of humanity does not? This is a particularly poignant question in light of the millions of people today who are displaced, have no home, are on the move, or are being forced out of even places of temporary belonging.

I believe that as part of life all people deal with what I call *ontological suffering*. We suffer because we are conscious beings aware that we are dying, and what and who we are is impermanent. If we are lucky, we experience our bodies aging, and we know that death awaits us. We love and then see many of those we love suffer and die. The world changes and becomes a less familiar place. All of this happens as part of life.

But we need not also be hungry or cold. We need not also be afraid of our neighbors. We need not also be told by our government that our lives don't matter because of our race, our gender, or our disability. These indignities are distinct from ontological suffering. *Surplus suffering* is not a necessary part of life.

In fact, if we could truly share our ontological suffering, we could lessen the sting of our surplus suffering.

Belonging, bridging, turning toward one another instead of against one another may not completely remove the disquiet of being an animal that knows we are dying, but they can certainly make it better.

I hope I have made it clear that *belonging* is nuanced and happens across many different domains. This complexity is compounded by the reality that there are a number of ways of thinking about belonging and there are many different areas, be it work or politics or community, where the concern for belonging is present. Home is one of our first sites of belonging, both metaphorically and literally. For some of us, it is at our place of worship or in nature. For some, it might be at our school or being with our close friends.

I am focusing on our goal of belonging without othering, but it is important to note some more negative ways of thinking about belonging exist. I already touched on the problem of the need to belong being used to promote othering. Another concern is that belonging can be a way of overpowering or destroying the individual. This expression assumes that the individual can exist only by being separate. I have suggested that what many Americans fear about Social Security is the social aspect of being tied to someone else, being dependent on and especially interdependent with the other.

A fear of the *other* is reproduced over and over. The fear is not just of lost material standing and status but also of defilement. During segregation in the US, this obsession gave us separate swimming pools, separate drinking fountains, and separate places to commune with the divine.

Any system organized around purity is a system organized around a narrow concept of belonging and is therefore deeply fragile. Consider the notion that one drop of something called Black blood could destroy the purity of whiteness.

To challenge this purity story is not just to challenge the structure of otherness and the myth of the pure *we* but to dislodge an ontological threat. One does not have to look far to find roots of this formative story in politics, science, law, and religion. Under such a configuration, the other will never be pure, and we will remain small, scared, and ready to fight for our group's purity. The fear of Blacks against the apparent purity of whiteness gave us the one drop rule. The assumption was that one drop of Black blood would destroy whiteness. Today we continue to hear this in relationship to immigrants and others.

So what, if anything, must change if we are truly to build belonging without othering?

We must first let go of the myth that bringing in the other to cocreate our shared world will not produce change. It will. But this should not make us smug or sanguine, as in, "We are willing to change, but they are not." We are all situated differently, and we will experience change differently. But in the spirit of bridging, we must be willing to listen to the underlying fear of change. We must believe there is room for all of us but not for domination or erasure of the other. Our belonging cannot be built on the other's not belonging.

Calling for cocreation is an essential part of belonging and bridging. And while it is a radical concept and may introduce anxiety, it is already present in the concept of democracy and equality. One mistaken assumption that is often made in the discussion of cocreation is that the old group is losing out and the new group is empowered to impose its will. But this is not what true belonging means. No group should be empowered to impose only its will. Each group should have the opportunity to participate and state its needs and become part of the shared space.

As we move more deeply into belonging and bridging, we begin to see that it is not just about our winning or losing but about caring and sharing in our collective and individual humanity.

Let me end this chapter with an assertion.

I am calling for a world where all belong and none are other. I am not calling for purity. Belonging may not be a destination but an orientation.

Let me state this more strongly. Even if we cannot completely imagine what belonging without othering is, I believe there is a good reason to use this ideal as an aspiration. This and related aspirations and practices should orient our behavior and anchor our evolving norms globally.

I assert that all people belong and should be accorded all the dignity and respect that flow from that. Despite much evidence to the contrary, we believe this assertion is or should be self-evident.

Reflect

- Take a moment and dream. What is a space within which you want to feel belonging? What does belonging look like to you in this space?

- Close your eyes for a moment and take a deep breath. Think about a place or situation where you have felt belonging. Now ground that feeling in your body, noticing your senses. What did that place or situation sound like? What did it feel like? Look like?

- What kind of belonging could we each cultivate in the areas we inhabit? What might this look like a year from now?

- What changes would you be willing to make to make the spaces you inhabit ones so that everyone could experience a sense of belonging?

- Take some time to think about what it means to create beyond-human belonging in your community.

7

Understanding Bridging

So how does bridging relate to our aspiration of belonging? While belonging is about our orientation, bridging is about *practices and values* that anchor us to those practices. Bridging is one of the most powerful ways that we can move *toward* our aspiration of belonging.

Bridging invites us to listen for the other person's story and particularly their suffering but also *their* aspirations and dreams. Bridging means we recognize that whatever is the key to the tension between us and the other is never the whole story. We are always more than our worst fears or worst acts. We yearn for our better angels and our best selves.

Bridging is in some sense a way to connect with the other. At a different level, bridging is also a way to connect with the earth and with the divine.

But what if the other does not want to bridge and does not want to connect? That might suggest a reason to not offer to bridge. Still, as James Baldwin states, we are helplessly and forever a part of each other. This is true even if we find that truth inconvenient. If the other refuses to bridge and accept our humanity, so be it. This does mean we are not connected, just not recognized.

Some will not bridge unless it is reciprocated and the conditions are right. This makes sense on a number of levels. Yet this position is a denial of what is and must be even if it goes unrecognized.

The other may have a different position than we do on any number of issues. But they probably also love their family and want the best for them, very much like us. Can we stay open and curious about not just their position but also their story and, even more fundamentally, their humanity?

Can we tell our own story as a bridging instead of a breaking story? Remember, a breaking story is where we believe the other shows up with only a single story, or is a threat, or is in competition with our story. In a bridging story, even as I lift my suffering, there is room to listen to your suffering as well.

Just as there are many ways to divide and break, there are many ways to bridge. Bridging reconnects us across divides, not just between hostile groups, but also within our own group and even within ourselves.

So where and how do we start with bridging? Of course, the answer to where you start is always the same. You start where you are. But let me make some additional suggestions. We start with being grounded in our intentions and, where appropriate, it may be useful to state these intentions to ourselves and the other person. Seeing the humanity in others does not entail denying or lessening one's own humanity. Listening to anyone does not mean giving up one's own story. It does not mean agreement.

Bridging is not about listening analytically to pick apart the other person's story; rather, it means to try to be more present with their feelings, their fears, and their suffering. We might be challenged by a situation and even articulate that, but we can still respond with wanting to hear the other person's situation. "Listening to you doesn't mean I agree, but I do want to try to see you as something bigger than the space where we differ."

It may not always be appropriate to state this intention to others, but it is important to be clear to yourself what your intentions are and are not. But once your intentions are articulated to yourself or to others, how might we explore bridging?

There may be times and situations where you or the other are not ready to bridge. Do threats exist that might undermine the possibility of bridging? The level of engagement also matters—is this an effort between just a few people or between groups? That can make the intervention and response more or less challenging, or challenging in different ways.

Let's discuss some of these dynamics related to bridging.

Bridging and Power

Much of the work related to bridging in the United States was influenced by the sociologist Robert Putnam. In famous works such as *Bowling Alone*, Putnam assumed that bridging would take place between two groups of relatively equal power, because he was concerned that extremely unequal power could distort bridging.

The more powerful group may have less incentive to bridge. Less powerful groups may have a greater need to bridge, because they do not have power to push their agenda; and at the same time they *also* may be less willing to bridge, because they are already the more vulnerable of the two groups.

These dynamics are tragically on display in Richard Wright's 1940 novel *Native Son* and comedically on display in the popular 2019 movie *Knives Out*. In the film, the character Marta Cabrera is a Latina caregiver for the elderly patriarch of a rich white family. Marta's mother is an undocumented immigrant. In one scene, the white family is having a debate about what should be "done" with undocumented immigrants. At some point they turn to ask Marta her opinion. Some of the family members are apparently aware that this might be a difficult situation for Marta. Can she express herself truthfully and disagree with her arrogant employer? She dodges the question. While they are not aware of her mother's situation, it's also clear they are not really that interested in her opinion. She lacks power and influence; to them, she lacks voice. In such a situation, it is not likely she can create a bridge toward them nor that they are interested in bridging with her.

In *Native Son*, a young Black man, Bigger Thomas, is hired to be a driver for a rich white family. When the daughter, Mary, returns home from college, she insists on riding in the front with Bigger. He is very uncomfortable with Mary in the front, and yet she refuses to recognize the power dynamics that cause his discomfort. In one point in the book, Mary insists that Bigger drive her and her boyfriend to a place where Bigger goes to eat. When they enter, she and her boyfriend are the only white people present. Bigger is extremely ill at ease. Without giving away the entire book, I will say that tragedy follows. In *Native Son*, power matters, and it also matters differently for those with a great deal of it and those with much less of it.

One of the insights we can take from recognizing that power can distort relations is that the onus of bridging should fall on the more powerful. And it is often assumed that less powerful groups do not need to be open to bridging because of their perceived lack of power. But there are a number of problems with a position that suggests less powerful groups should not bridge. Of course, no one can be compelled to bridge. But we must be careful not to overuse the power issue as a reason not to bridge. In most cases, the power imbalance between groups will not be so extreme that bridging cannot happen.

When we think of power differentials, we often think about it at the level of groups. For example, whites may be thought of as having more power than nonwhites, and collectively speaking this is accurate. But power is much more situational. To understand the power dynamic, one must consider the immediate environment and not just history or aggregated power. Even for a group who has been injured and has diminished power or resources, I believe it is still important to be open to bridging.

In fact, groups who have been the objects of much breaking and othering are likely to engage in breaking themselves, not just with the more powerful but with peer groups and less powerful groups.

However, while this may feel good in the moment, it is not likely to produce constructive results.

Breaking can become habit-forming, with no logical stopping place. A number of articles and studies have shone attention on breaking within organizations among people who appear to have similar goals and values. A widely discussed 2022 article from *The Forge* called "Building Resilient Organizations," from strategist and activist Maurice Mitchell, spoke to the increased breaking and fragmentation in the social, grassroots, and nonprofit sectors. Mitchell named ways we can not only confront how we are breaking but also lean into care and compassion in order to withstand the inevitable small breaks and fractures. It is notable that none of these require us to abandon our position on any number of issues, including racial and social equality for all.

When groups and society overall become caught up in cycles of breaking, there are negative effects both for society and for the groups engaged in the breaking. Although it may be apparent that suggesting a marginal group not bridge would be a way to relieve them from a burden, such a suggestion is more likely to limit both their ability to heal and the full expression of their humanity. To state this another way: a group being othered can turn around and *other* another less powerful group; the assumption that they would automatically show empathy or solidarity is incorrect.

One must be willing to consider power and its importance to support the needed conditions for bridging. But one must be careful not to call for exact symmetry in power or to point to power differences in a generalized way; it's important to attend to the nuances of what is happening in a concrete situation.

There are those who may belong, but their belonging is highly conditional, with conditions set by the supposed true *we*. For example, let's take the story that women may belong, but only under the supervision of a man. Under this arrangement, there may even be love in both directions. You may note the power arrangement in this example: one group is setting the terms for the other. But this is also stated too starkly and is too reductive. While the power difference is real and consequential, it is virtually never the complete story. One group or person may be more dominant than another, but not in every situation.

Just as in the example of my parents and me, or women and men, or Black and white people, there is always power on both sides, even though it may be far from equal. Some, including the Supreme Court, argued that antimiscegenation laws and mores could not be racist, as the rule applied to whites and nonwhites equally, and therefore did not violate the principle of equality as stated in the Fourteenth Amendment. A later court struck down these laws, noting that they were not in fact expressions of equality but of white supremacy. Even at the time that the Supreme Court was adopting the Jim Crow ideology of *separate but equal*, one of the dissenting justices noted that there was a power difference inherent in this decision.

So belonging holds the claim that there is no natural *other*. And yet in our current reality there are others, and there is othering. Society has made this so; it has also determined that the power to make and define is not equally distributed. Since it is a social process, we have the power to change and effectively end it.

Thinking in terms of groups helps us to learn to bridge—or, maybe more accurately, to build a particular type of bridge. When there is breaking at the group level, part of the work that breaking is doing is to secure one's sense of belonging in one's group. When thinking about cleavages between institutions and even nations, we can see how this function of breaking is compounded: in such situations there is likely to be positive regard for breaking with the out-group and protection of the in-group.

People are moved to bridge or break not just because of their own individual concerns but often in order to get or stay in good standing with a group that is important to them. The in-group has the power to discipline members to stay in line. "If you bridge with that other group, you might be kicked out. Where is your loyalty?"

If I reach out to another group, I might lose my belonging in my group that defines and sustains me as well as not gain standing in the other group. I run the risk of becoming groupless. For most of us, this would be a serious problem. In bridging we often face a heightened degree of vulnerability, perhaps even arguably an existential threat, such as in the case of our earlier example with Socrates.

When I was in high school in Detroit, it was understood that there were cool and not cool students, a fact that I'm sure has not changed today. At that time there was even a popular Motown song called "The 'In' Crowd." Everyone wanted to be part of the in crowd. I liked to read a lot, and being seen with books was a badge of not being in the in crowd. I developed elaborate patterns so that I could do my homework and read without transporting books between school and home. At some level I wanted to be part of the in crowd, while I also wanted to engage in activities that placed me squarely outside of the in crowd. I hid my desire to learn and read in the hopes that if it stayed hidden, I could then belong. Nonetheless, I never did become part of the in crowd, and while I would like to think it didn't matter, it did. It both mattered and did not matter and sometimes both at the same time. I was on the periphery of the in crowd. And I am not proud to say that I had friends whom I othered because they were considered outside the in crowd.

Virtually all groups can exact pressure on its members to conform. The *New York Times* columnist David Brooks, who identifies politically as a moderate conservative, has written about being subject to these dynamics. I would call him not just a person who engages in bridging but a person who is a bridger. Brooks, who founded the group Weave at the Aspen Institute, has written a lot on the urgent need to bridge and why. Weavers not only consider opinions on the other side but show a willingness to consider the other's humanity even in disagreement.

Following the 2016 US election, as the country and political formations accelerated fracturing and people were separating and taking sides, Brooks wrote about finding himself in between groups. As he was being pushed from his own in-group, he was not being embraced by the other. He has written about his work from an ethical citizen's sense of doing the right and necessary thing. He has discussed the importance of staying open to one another not just in order to make better decisions but to claim our full humanity. I read his position as often bordering on the spiritual. Still, there may have been a sting that he was not prepared for. He has shared publicly about some of the social isolation he was experiencing. I found my eleven-year-old self feeling compassion for his suffering.

This is one of the ways groups enact discipline: they limit fellowship. There are often unwritten rules that, when broken, have durable consequences. When one continues to consider the role of the group, both the power of and the challenges to bridging come into sharper focus.

Complexity and Multiplicity

I stated earlier that breaking is founded on anxiety and fear and a simplified story about the other, where the other is not a complex human but a caricature that must be contained, constrained, exploited, or flattened. I am explicitly promoting that we engage *complexity* in order to bridge.

What is the other's story of themselves as well as their story of us? We need to start there. *Us versus them* is very simple. But *we and we* is full of complexity and surprises and will continue to change until we die. Can we get to a bigger *us* story instead of *us versus them*? To listen to the other's story, we need curiosity and a willingness to engage complexity. Because people are both complex and always changing, we should not expect to fully understand them or even ourselves. Bridging calls on us not only to understand but also, and possibly more importantly, to feel.

Why is complexity more likely to promote bridging than simplicity? As I mentioned earlier, we are made of multiple selves. Think of Walt Whitman's phrase "I contain multitudes." If I can access both my multiplicity and some of the multiplicity of the other, I open up more possibilities of places for us to connect.

This is captured beautifully in the Baldwin quote I shared earlier about each of us containing the other. Baldwin in *Here Be Dragons* stated, "We are all androgynous, not only because we are all born of a woman impregnated by the seed of a man but because each of us, helplessly and forever, contains the other."

We are a part of each other, Baldwin insisted. And so do I.

Bridging becomes more likely to occur if we can lean into the many identities we carry. In addition to such a space offering more possibilities to connect, in this space we may be less prone to fear and anxiety. The other may be different and at odds with me on some or even many things, but if I remain open to exploring our multiplicities, we have a much greater chance to find or create space where we can bridge, with or without agreement. Someone might be a racist, a homophobe, or an espouser of other bigoted beliefs. But if we engage complexity, we will find that no one is *just* that one thing.

A more complicated person seen in a more complicated story is easier to bridge with. Engaging complexity is not just about finding existing common ground, it is also about creating new possibilities and new common ground.

Too much in our culture pushes us toward simplicity. Of course, we all want to pull for the "good guy" and condemn the evil one. But this life and the people in it are not so straightforward.

Consider a few movies that illustrate this point. Let's start with Ryan Coogler's 2018 superhero film *Black Panther*. Who was the good guy, and who was the bad guy? For me, the brilliance of the movie is that the hero, Black Panther, and his seeming antagonist, Erik Killmonger, were both admirable *and* flawed characters. Many people left the movie feeling conflicted about whom to root for. I suggest that is a good thing.

Another example is the classic movie directed by Spike Lee, *Do the Right Thing*, which I recently rewatched and appreciated even more now than when I first saw it twenty-five years ago. The protagonists of *Do the Right Thing* are Sal, an Italian American who owns and operates a pizzeria in a predominantly Black Brooklyn neighborhood, and Mookie, played by Spike Lee, who works for Sal delivering pizzas. Another central character is Radio Raheem, whose name refers to the radio he carries wherever he goes.

The plot builds to a central scene where, after rising tensions, Radio Raheem comes into Sal's pizzeria with his music blasting. When Sal hears the song "Fight the Power" by Public Enemy blaring inside his establishment, he receives it not just as a physical assault but as an attack on the sanctity of his restaurant. Sal demands that Radio turn the music down in *his* restaurant; Radio Raheem turns it up. Sal gets a bat and destroys the radio. As a crowd assembles in protest outside the pizzeria, Mookie picks up a trash can and throws it through the window, inciting the assembled group to torch Sal's restaurant. Radio Raheem attacks Sal, the police arrive, and they kill Radio Raheem.

While the movie has a number of storylines, I was especially drawn to the conflicted, layered relationship between Sal and Mookie. It was full of bridges and love, on one hand, and of breaking, on the other. I found the characters to be multidimensional and complex.

Who is the villain and who is the hero in *Do the Right Thing*? Even as the protagonists keep reaching for each other, they continue to come up short. Try as they might on an interpersonal level, they can never fully get beyond the shadow of racism, which acts as an ongoing break. Locked in their own grievances, Sal and Mookie miss opportunities to bridge.

I saw the real perpetrator in *Do the Right Thing* as a system that has pitted the lives of these characters against each other, despite their love that refuses to stay inside society's defined boundaries. Throughout the movie, the neighborhood police see their role as primarily one of protecting the white people and their property while overpolicing the Black community. The police and the state worked to restore belonging for Sal, but not for the Black members in their own neighborhood. The belonging of the two groups is portrayed by the state in a zero-sum manner, and the power afforded to the groups is very asymmetrical.

The film also illustrates how breaking at the individual level, which happens between many of the characters, does not have the same consequences as the reach of the state: the unarmed Black man Radio Raheem ends up dead. The movie reads like an earlier plea for Black lives to matter.

Complexity in Framing

I want to continue to explore complexity as we learn how to bridge.

Let's look at some generalized frames around political and social positions. When *conservatives versus liberals* are set up as opposing forces, it is often assumed that the conservative is trying to hold onto the old ways and the liberal, or progressive, is supporting change and progress. A value is implicit in this formulation: from a liberal perspective, the value that promotes change and progress is seen as good, while the value that supports the old ways and status quo is seen as out of touch and bad.

Several problems arise with this frame. As we discussed earlier, while change will happen, in and of itself change is value neutral. There can be changes for the better as well as changes for the worse. In our example of Trump and Obama, one could claim that Trump's call for change was past-looking and Obama's was largely future-facing. Is this the difference—that the past stands for bad and the future stands for good? Not necessarily. More to the point, all of us can handle only so much rapid change in a short time before it can become destructive; this is true whether we think of the change as good or bad.

We need a balance between change and stability. Most people would probably agree, but getting agreement on the right balance may not be so easy.

Part of that depends on how the change or stability will affect us. Consider coal miners. Would they agree that we should stop coal mining in order to switch to other types of energy sources? For those of us who are not miners, we may have little to lose and much to gain. But for coal mining communities, if switching energy sources means they would have to give up both their income and their way of life, one might expect some resistance. But what if the shift from coal is likely to greatly increase the cost of fuel for all? This change might also deeply impact non–coal miners.

When we look at how change or stability will impact someone's life, we should not be surprised to see a correlation between this impact and how much they support the change or status quo. There are some circumstances where any of us would be leery of a change and some where any of us would support the status quo.

As discussed earlier, it is not enough to know what someone's stance is on a position. It is also important to understand how they are situated in the world and how they make meaning of that situatedness. When I was growing up and someone was challenged to not only do something different but to be different, the response would often be "God is not done with you yet." This suggests the possibility and even the inevitability of change. Life demands, and is indeed a process of, change. But even though life calls for change, it will feel different when the change is being called for and enforced by a group that one is not a part of. That change can easily be experienced as domination.

When we like the changes we are making, we call it growth or progress. When we don't like the changes, we describe it as loss or disruption. Rapid change can overwhelm the most flexible and secure among us. And yet the effort to completely stop change is self-defeating and life denying.

These insights are important as we approach bridging. I suggested earlier that the speed of change can exacerbate our anxiety and fear. Underlying this is the sense that we are rapidly moving to a world where we do not fit in, and it is a world not of our making. Much fear and anxiety is about not fitting in or belonging.

Practices of bridging and breaking have many different expressions, and those dynamics are often laced with complexity. Properly understood and engaged, complexity is our friend for the project of bridging. Complexity calls on us to be curious about people in general.

There is a saying: Because we are both the same and different, dialogue is necessary and possible. If we were just different, then dialogue would not be possible. If we were just the same, dialogue would not be necessary.

Sacred Symbols

Another one of the most powerful ways to bridge or break is through sacred symbols. Robert Sapolsky has made the observation that many conflicts and even wars are fought over sacred symbols. Groups engaging in overt breaking are likely to resort to denigrating sacred symbols to insult and dehumanize the other. These efforts are not random attacks: they are meant to cut deeply into the essence of what the other group finds worthy.

But what is a sacred symbol, and what makes it so? There is the obvious example of something of profound meaning and reverence in a religious context, such as the cross in Christianity or the wheel of the law in Buddhism. A symbol is sacred because it touches something deep inside of us. It helps to give our life meaning. These symbols in many ways represent our connection to the divine or something larger than ourselves.

Sacred symbols are often religious or spiritual but need not necessarily be. And it is usually not the symbol itself but rather our relationship to the symbol that makes it sacred, even in a nonreligious context. When the relationship to that symbol is shared by others over time, it is even more powerful.

Sacred symbols often represent a collective expression. A holy icon or ritual becomes sacred because the congregants treat it as sacred. It is an agreement embodied in a practice and meaning that both reflects and personifies the individual or group while at the same time transcending the person and group.

There are often ritual and shared practices around sacred symbols. To denigrate someone's sacred symbol is to denigrate their grounding in the soul.

If one of the ways to engage in serious breaking is to denigrate another's sacred symbols, then, by the same token, one of the ways to bridge is to acknowledge the other's sacred symbols.

There is personal symbolism as well as collective. When I was growing up in Detroit, one of the unofficial sacred symbols in my neighborhood was one's mother. If one person called out a negative trait about another, the response "Your mama" quickly and unreflectively meant, "Prepare to fight." Our teachers would try to stop us by saying something ridiculous like, "Words don't matter. You can't fight each other just because someone said something about your mother." What our teachers did not or chose not to realize was that the person had crossed a line much more serious than a physical punch. And if you did not respond, not only would you be disrespecting your mother, you would also lose credibility in your community. Even if you knew you could not win the physical fight, fighting was what you had to do. Wasn't it Socrates who made the point that there are some things worse than physical death? *Not belonging* might be one of them.

To return to the film *Do The Right Thing*, many of the struggles between the protagonists play out through sacred symbols. When Sal's restaurant is attacked, the injury to him is not just over his property. It comes after much pushback about the display of Italian American photos on the wall, symbols of his pride in his ethnic heritage. Sal's pride is experienced by many Black patrons as an attack and a sign of disrespect. Sal may not have meant any disrespect in hanging only photos of Italian Americans on his wall. But the call for the pictures to change becomes a threat to his most important identity, that of an Italian American. A struggle arises over what those mean in the context of the place where the pizzeria is located.

Similarly, in the pivotal scene where Sal tells Radio Raheem he just killed Raheem's radio, we know that a radio has no life. But Sal knows at some level, just like we the viewers do, that Raheem's radio not only had life but that its life was tied to something that was sacred to Radio Raheem. His very name speaks of his connection with his radio.

The film continually weaves in how sacred symbols act as vectors of both othering and belonging. Sacred symbols don't just act independently; they are also wrapped up in the relationships the characters have with each other, the bridges and love that have been built.

When change is demanded of Sal by others in the neighborhood, the situation is complicated by feelings and history. What feels like what I call a *short bridge* becomes a breaking moment with very real consequences. When Sal gets the state involved, as I recounted earlier, the stakes become much higher and even deadly, but only for some. I will go into more detail about long and short bridges later in the book.

The meanings bestowed by sacred symbols set real conditions in the world. Several years ago, I was offered a professorship at a school in the American South. The conditions and the remuneration were all attractive. The people were warm and engaged. During the interview process at the university, as we walked around to tour the beautiful campus, I saw several signs and symbols glorifying the Confederacy of the Civil War. My host hastily assured me that although this state had fought on the side of the seceding South, those symbolic reminders had little meaning today.

This statement was not reassuring to me. The Confederate symbolism sent a strong message that I interpreted as not only I but Black people in general did not belong on this campus.

I did not take the offered position.

The simple story that was told by the monuments to a Civil War South did not reflect my experience as either an individual or as a Black American at the group level. It might be more accurate to say these symbols *did* in fact reflect an experience for me, but one that was very different from that of my white host. While I can accept that those were not meaningful anymore to the school or to him, in some way it made it all the more disturbing that they remained, as if they were empty containers that meant nothing. The meaning he invited me to have—one of *not* assigning a meaning to their continued display on the campus—was not available or desirable to me.

The story those symbols told me was that in this space, there was a continuation of othering.

Experiences like these are fraught when a positive symbol for one group is experienced as a direct affront to another group. Can there be a positive meaning to a Confederate flag that is not associated with the enslavement of Black people? Is the flag so deeply tied to racial domination that whatever else it might mean is overwhelmed by this core association? Sacred symbols matter. Recognizing or attacking the sacred or the symbolic carries an extra weight. It involves a deep kind of breaking. And what if the very purpose of a sacred symbol is to mark the domination and subhuman status of the other?

When is it appropriate to recognize the sacred symbols of others we are in conflict with? Consider the case of apartheid South Africa. The language of Afrikaans and the game of rugby were both considered culturally sacred for white Afrikaners. But Afrikaans was experienced as an insult by many Black South Africans. When it was mandated as the language of instruction in schools, many Black South Africans protested. Yet during this same time, Nelson Mandela, who was imprisoned, asked his prison guards to teach him Afrikaans. Mandela was aware of both the controversy around and the importance of the language. When Mandela was released from prison and was elected president of South Africa, one of the first things he did was attend a rugby match where the South African team was playing for the world championship. He was exceedingly aware of the symbolism of rugby and of who it spoke to.

Mandela used the honoring of both symbols to create a bridge between Black and white South Africans. One might add that Mandela not only honored these sacred symbols, but he also changed their meaning. His acknowledgment of these sacred cultural symbols also built a bridge between the past and the potential future of South Africa—one that had not arrived yet, though he created the possibility for it to arrive.

Some people, even today, feel that Mandela should not have constructed this bridge. Was this a slight to South African Black people?

Was this a bridge too long? That is up to each of us to decide. But to recognize that shared symbols might have very different meanings for different groups is part of bridging. I will return later to this question of long bridges and the role of leaders to construct bridges in ways that may not be available to all of us.

Situatedness

Earlier, I discussed *situatedness* as it relates to othering and breaking. Here I will reexamine situatedness as it relates to bridging. Appreciating how we are each situated differently can be a source for bridging. Many of our interests and even values are what they are because of our situatedness. And we may create an other because of different situatedness.

There are many parts of us that influence how we experience life and how the world views us. A person doesn't have just a race (or mix of races) but also a gender, sexual orientation, religion, party affiliation—or not.

To think only of someone's race, for example, may often be to think of too little. The critical race theorist Kimberlé Crenshaw popularized the term *intersectionality*, which in part illuminates the fact that the way a Black woman and a Black man experience the world, and the way the world sees them, is likely to be very different. There is an intersection of race and gender and many other traits.

The very concept of our identities points to what I earlier called our *situatedness*. Both intersectionality and situatedness may help us to better understand how identities work. But the reality is that we are not just talking about fixed things like race or gender; we are talking about dynamic processes and meanings that shift over time.

I use the term situatedness as a formal way of saying that everyone has multiple stories, and these stories are important to understanding who we are intrinsically and who we are in relation to one another. It is not just that we have different sets of experiences, but that these interactions also have an energy attached to them and a meaning. Our situatedness in a larger public story might hide that we are all composites of many things; and in turn those things will have different implications to us and to others, depending on situatedness. Our experiences themselves are given meaning through structures and cultures. It a mistake to think of experiences as direct and unmediated.

Iris Young, a brilliant political philosopher, brings clarity to the issue of situatedness. She notes that virtually all politics are identity politics in that they focus on the concerns of particular populations in particular situations. Then she adds an important twist: most of what people are concerned about under the frame of identity politics is in fact situational or structural. Farmers are likely to oppose limits on food exportation because it will impact them in the export market, not because they are farmers. Women's issues are issues that more likely will impact them because of how they are situated in our society, not because they are women. She applies the same logic to issues related to race and other concerns. What is important about her observation is that she moves us away from focusing on something inside the individual or group and instead toward focusing on their conditions and contexts. If you change the conditions of a group, one would then expect their interests and values to also change. This creates more possibilities for groups both to come together and to be remade.

The social meanings of our own traits in the world will also have a great deal to do with how we experience them. When we are threatened on the basis of a particular trait of ours, such as our religion or race, that trait is likely to become more salient to us. But if the threat to our identity is removed, the importance of the trait is likely to subside.

Too often, we will be threatened and then told that the source of the threat should have little meaning to us by the very group that is causing the threat. Another way to say this is that when breaking happens along a particular axis, the trait associated with that axis is likely to take on more importance. I am a tall Black man. On a work trip, I was walking through the lobby of a hotel on my way to my room. I was stopped by security and asked what my business was in the hotel.

The question felt to me more like a statement than an inquiry: "Are you up to no good?" The implied meaning was: "You (and your kind) do not belong here." I didn't witness anyone else being stopped in the busy space of a large hotel.

To some extent the question became self-fulfilling. Before the encounter with the security guard, I did feel like I belonged in the hotel, but once the question was asked, on some level I no longer felt as if I belonged.

A few hours later, I left the hotel to go to the venue where I was invited to give a keynote talk, which was the reason for my trip. Upon entering, I was greeted warmly as "Professor powell." The space extended was one of belonging.

Was I the person in the hotel lobby or the one at the lectern?

What I'm suggesting is that our identities rely in large part on our situatedness in social contexts. When those contexts or our situatedness changes, then our identities will also experience change.

In a series of conversations between James Baldwin and anthropologist Margaret Mead in 1970, Baldwin asked Mead about her experience being a woman in anthropology, a field heavily populated with men. He asked her if she ever felt out of place. Mead responded that as a white woman from England and a highly regarded scholar, she felt like she belonged everywhere.

When she turned the question to Baldwin, perhaps expecting a similar response from this highly acclaimed writer, Baldwin instead stated that as a Black and gay man in America, there was no place where he felt like he belonged.

We can learn much in this exchange. It asks the question "Which of our identities will be the most important to us in each situation?" Not only, like Baldwin and Mead, do we have many identities, but our identities are activated across situations differently. It might have been for Mead that her status as a white English anthropologist allowed her to belong in most, if not all, situations. But for Baldwin, being Black and gay in America in 1970 easily overwhelmed any status gained from being a renowned writer. Mead belonging everywhere also reflected her being the citizen of a dominant colonial power at that time. This power may be bestowed on people without them asking for it, but it is bestowed nonetheless.

I have good friends who were in an interracial relationship. He is a medical worker and white; she is a professor and Taiwanese. My friends lived in a town with few Asians. Frequently when in public they experienced possible slights. For example, the waiter would come to them after serving people who had arrived after them, or they would not be given eating utensils. My female friend would interpret these interactions as racial slights. Her partner always assumed there must be an innocent explanation. He went so far as to insist that even if they were racial slights, his wife should not let them bother her. It is difficult to know if the slights were racial or not. But it does say something that the white male could not see the *possibility* that these incidents might have had racial undertones, nor did he think it important enough to believe the person he loved the most in the world. Not only are we likely to be treated differently in the world, depending how we are perceived, but we are also likely to interpret what happens to us through a filter of who we are and what groups we are associated with. My friends ended up divorcing.

This subtle dynamic is important as we think about bridging and belonging. We cannot ask the marginalized group to participate by ignoring the very thing we use to limit their participation. Asking for or insisting on a marginalized group to stop identifying and join a seemingly neutral space, one where they (but not we) check their identity at the door, is itself a form of breaking. We are saying, "I can only empathize with you and your situation if it is the same as mine."

Situatedness can help us notice, without getting lost in essentialism, how different groups are dealing with different environments and conditions. The reason women are not likely to be truck drivers is not because of the "inherent nature" of women, but because of how we have created policy, space, and a story about where women (and men) belong.

In the earlier example about James Baldwin, his race and his being gay were more important, at least in some contexts, than him being an acclaimed writer or a US citizen. One might also ask: Did Baldwin decide the importance of his race and sexual orientation, or did the larger society? Mead seems to be suggesting that her gender was of less salience than her being white, English, and a well-known anthropologist. Her situatedness allowed her access that Baldwin was not afforded. Were these their decisions or the larger society's?

Othering and breaking are constitutive, meaning they impact how we experience life and our way of acting and seeing the world. Most of us probably fall somewhere between Mead and Baldwin. Few of us feel that we belong everywhere, and few of us feel like we are othered everywhere.

In a world where we feel a sense of belonging in some places and a sense of othering in other places, we are inclined to try to move toward the belonging spaces. If women feel like they do not belong in spaces where men are likely to dominate, they may attempt to avoid those spaces, narrowing the opportunities represented in those spaces.

This is one of the many dangers of segregation and separation. When a group feels safer in a space where life chances are constrained, that reality contains its own kind of peril. The insidiousness of the concept of knowing and staying in one's place comes to mind.

We seek spaces and places to belong for many reasons. But as Mead and Baldwin suggested, she feels she belongs everywhere, and he feels he belongs nowhere. How do we increase spaces and places where we can all belong?

One of the ongoing discussions today in the Black community in the US is whether Black people should avoid being in predominantly white spaces for their own safety. This represents a paradox. Racial segregation imposes a high cost without providing safety. As Maslow noted in the pyramid of our needs, we need to belong to have safety. Segregation denies that.

Segregated spaces do not just cut a group off from other groups; they also segregate the group off from opportunity.

While it may be understandable for a group to try to retreat from public and shared spaces, it is very doubtful that segregation and retreat can provide either safety or opportunity. Segregation is imposed on a people for the benefit of a different people. When deeply othered people are under constant surveillance but seldom truly seen, it may be understandable for them to try to retreat, but is still problematic. Segregation is about hoarding or segregating opportunities and benefits. It is not only or even primarily about the location of people. When nonwhites were or are separated from their white counterparts geographically, that spatial separation also means the uneven and unequal distribution of financial, educational, and other resources. We should not be surprised that once people in this country were segregated, redlining and the segregation of money followed. When there is no hoarding of material benefits on the basis of space or geography, the reason for segregation becomes moot.

We use public space to distribute many of society's benefits, including the making of social norms and markets. The German sociologist Max Weber warned against abandoning the public space to a perceived safer inner space. Weber was concerned with the internal space that one retreats to becoming smaller and smaller, while the external (public) space is left to others to construct and dominate. Both spaces become distorted. And the inner space will still be defined by the group that controls the outer space. Ultimately, the inner space becomes so small that it cannot support a full self.

This becomes an extreme version of what happens to virtually all of us. As infinite spirits, we are often frustrated in finding full expressions of ourselves while in finite bodies. But again, a healthy solution cannot be to retreat. A retreat may temporarily spare us some harm, but it is already inflicting another kind of harm.

A few concrete examples might be useful. In the US and much of the world, until the 1900s women were consigned largely to private space, and men controlled and populated public space. This not only cut women off from all the resources that were distributed and arranged in public spaces, but it also gave men the right to define the role of women in both public and private spaces. In early domestic violence cases, the state would often refuse to intervene, as such matters were seen as private. Women could not easily escape such situations, since men controlled the finances of the family. It has been said the home was the man's castle and the woman's dungeon.

Another telling example is found in the US housing market. The modern housing market was formed in the 1930s and '40s, when the federal government created a number of policies to make mortgages available to much of America. However, this seemingly public market was not accessible on the same terms to any women, Black Americans, or Jewish Americans. As is set out by Douglas Massey in *Categorically Unequal*, these public policies consigned nonwhites and nonmales to a segregated space. The segregation consisted not just of the separation of people but also of the separating of opportunity.

This reality allowed white men both to accumulate wealth and to hoard wealth and opportunity. Wealth, which is a major vehicle to other goods and services, like schools, health care, and jobs, was deeply racialized and gendered.

In response, some have called upon Black groups and other isolated groups to embrace their forced isolation and instead fend for themselves in separate spaces. Such a call ignores the fact that when the private sphere is cut off from the larger public sphere, it subjects the people in that segregated sphere to fewer and fewer resources. If by chance people in these segregated spaces find a way to thrive, they may be subject to direct attacks from the dominant society. This was the case in the 1921 Tulsa race massacre in Oklahoma, when a violent white supremacist mob destroyed a prosperous Black neighborhood known as Black Wall Street, killed or injured hundreds of residents, and left 10,000 people homeless.

It is not that segregated groups are helpless in situations such as redlining, but they are still impacted. In the case of trying to buy housing without the support of the federal government, other mechanisms were used by Black Americans, such as the land contract.

The house that I grew up in in Detroit was purchased under a land contract. When one buys a house through the bank with a mortgage, one immediately become the owner, albeit with the bank having interest. This means if the value of the house appreciates, that appreciation goes to the buyer. Under a land contract, however, the buyer does not get any interest in the property until the final payment. If the buyer misses a payment, the seller can keep all the payments and retake the house. (There are now some protections for the buyer under land contracts.) Land contracts greatly limited the ability of Black buyers to accumulate wealth. When my parents sold this house after living in it for more than fifty years and raising nine children, it sold for $5,000. It was estimated that if this house had been sold in the general housing market, it would have sold for over $200,000.

While this example is from the housing market, a similar tax is imposed on virtually all efforts by marginalized people to retreat to inner or segregated space or separate space. The inner and outer are connected, and as such no group should allow other groups to consign them to any smaller space. This speaks to one of the negative effects of stereotyping. A Black man is not allowed to be a bird-watcher. A woman is not allowed to be an omnipotent God. When we are consigned to a narrow inner and outer space, we are also likely to engage in self-policing and experience internal stereotype anxiety, or what social pychologist Claude Steele calls *stereotype threat*. In such a situation, one is unconsciously aware of being the other and possibly under surveillance. This can take away much energy and depress both one's performance and the ability to engage with life.

Belonging: Toward What Future?

Throughout the book, I frequently mention anxiety in response to a rapidly changing world. The threat of the other may be seen as a threat to our continuity. The autocratic leader assures us that they can stop this change and take control. They promise us a future that is a replica of a mythical past. In part they promise a future *without* change, a future where our belonging is secure and all threatening others will be removed or at least kept in their place.

Consider how often right-wing leaders call for a return to the glory, if not the structure, of the past. They say, "Let's make India/America/Russia great again." No matter that the time they envision never was and certainly will not be. But there is a preference for this mythical past in order to avoid an inevitable future. For many, sharing the world with the other is all but inconceivable.

One only has to look at popular cultural portrayals of the future to begin to understand why the authoritarian leader tries to console by offering to simply reinstate a fanciful past. The future that is most often presented is dystopian, where our world is no longer habitable, it's overrun with zombies and robots, and humans are on the run. In essence it's a world where humans do not belong.

That dystopian future does not have to be the inevitable future. That the world is ever-increasingly diverse and pluralist is inevitable. But it is not a given whether that world will offer a livable future based on belonging or not. That part is up to us. What we can know is that we are much better off facing this unknown future together instead of in opposition to one another.

Bridging and breaking also involve time. Our individual and collective beings and stories are distributed across time and space. To bridge with the future will require some bridging also with the present and the past. We need to find ways to bridge to a future where all belong and no groups are othered or dominated. If we survive, the future that comes will not be a replica of the past.

But we should not glibly assume that we can meet the future with confidence, without any anxiety, or that we can beat this anxiety through personal interventions alone. We all have our limits, which if pushed in excess will threaten the integrity of our being even if our limits are different from someone else's. We must prepare for the future, even as we can never be certain our preparation will be adequate. We need a new and better story, one that acknowledges the challenges and uncertainty that we face but also focuses on how working together, turning *to* each other instead of *on* each other, we will be more than fine.

Consciously and deliberately bridging toward a larger *we* is one of the best ways for us to help both make and prepare for the future. The future demands that we change. But this change will look different for different people. For example, we often assume that an older person's ability to adapt is more limited than a younger person's. We also often assume that a person with material resources is likely to have more capacity to adapt. Of course, any given person will have different abilities to adapt, depending on a myriad of variables. Scientist Jared Diamond studies what happens when different societies are called upon to make collective change for survival. He studies societies that are materially capable of making such changes, but he finds that most do not. Instead, these societies are likely to collapse, as his book *Collapse: How Societies Choose to Fail or Succeed* discusses.

Stress and anxiety about the present or the future are not likely to be evenly distributed. Different groups and communities, depending on their situatedness and context, will have differing capacities to adapt. Part of bridging, then, is to understand *how* we are differently situated. This requires recognizing that different groups will need different supports to come into the future as dignified, belonging people.

This not only means embracing multiple stories about *ourselves* but also embracing multiple complex stories about others who are situated differently and who have different sacred symbols and stories from ours.

Bridging by embracing our and others' situatedness opens up a sense of possibility amid change. It is easier to imagine changes in our environment than a notion that groups and individuals have an inherent unchanging nature. The latter is the claim of essentialism that drains the possibility of change and hope from our imagination, both for ourselves and for the other.

Accepting that many of our differences and interests are situational allows us to begin to recognize that some of the differences between people are explained by their environments and therefore are constantly subject to change.

The Nature of Change

It is not enough just to understand that change is inevitable. We must look more carefully at the speed of the change and its nature.

We are more likely to embrace change that we want or are calling for than change that is imposed on us. One person's progress or positive change can be another person's loss. Consider coal miners again, this time in the context of fossil fuels and jobs. If you are working in a space where your income is not visibly dependent on oil or coal, the cost of moving away from a dependency on fossil fuels may be of little consequence to you. It may be easier for you to advocate for a fossil-free world, since the impact on you will be small. But if you are a coal miner in the Appalachian Mountains and the coal industry shuts down, this future might mean not only a loss of employment but a loss of a complete way of life.

Our attachments to our place are not just attachments, they are part of who we are. The change or loss is about our being. Change will continue, but when it is imposed by others without our consent or without our grief being recognized, our response can easily become something more than anxiety. When our voices and concerns are not considered, we are likely to feel invisible or, worse, that our lives do not matter.

But if we begin to appreciate the pain that others may experience with change, we are likely to find a bridge even if the change is not problematic for us.

One of the injuries often associated with displacement is a sense of loss. The displacement doesn't have to be spatial; it can be displacement from a story and from a way of life. Our sense of well-being and belonging is personal, yes, but it is also tied to groups with which we identify. The burdens and benefits of change, and the embrace of or resistance to it, will vary a great deal. The movement of change is not just about material things and the environment, but also deeply about us. Our identities are made of experiences, stories, and places, with some being insignificant and others being very important. Many Indigenous communities refuse to leave their land, even in exchange for large monetary payments or other land. For many Indigenous communities, the expression "Mother Earth" is more than a metaphor. They experience the earth as a literal part of them, as their mother, their most intimate kin. How much would you sell your mother for?

We may not appreciate what we value until it is lost or threatened. Years ago, I moved to Minneapolis with my son. I bought a house in a friendly middle-class neighborhood. What I loved most about the house was a magnificent Dutch elm tree in my backyard. The tree had a canopy that extended beyond my yard to cover both neighboring yards. But the tree became diseased and eventually had to be removed. Even as I write this, I feel grief for the tree and for me. I considered moving from the house. The loss of the tree was painful and could not be alleviated by planting another tree.

We all have things in our individual and collective lives that are special and even sacred. To recognize someone, to bridge with someone, often requires that we recognize what they hold sacred.

I am not only talking about our individual experiences; we must look at our relational ones as well. We are all situated in relationship to one another. Too often we tend to think of our situatedness or our identities as stable and independent of other things. But both are always changing. Situatedness can mean the physical environment and the way space is constructed and who it's constructed for. An event held in a space without a ramp is a breaking space telling a breaking story. It sends a message that someone who needs a ramp does not really belong there. How do we design and engage spaces that bridge?

Understanding situatedness offers us a method of widening our view and how we see one another. We can enlarge this understanding by finding our common situatedness and by being curious about those who are differently situated than us.

Biologist and author Robert Sapolsky recounts a story of British commandos during World War II who captured a German general in the occupied island of Crete. Captors and captured stayed awake all night, waiting for the next stage of the plan, and together they saw the sunrise dawn over the mountainous landscape. The German general became fixated on the view and began to recite a poem in Latin. Listening to him, the British special agent who had coordinated the capture, Patrick Leigh Fermor, joined in to finish the recitation with the German general. In that moment, Fermor recounts in his memoir, something opened between them: "For five minutes the war had evaporated without a trace." Even if for just a few shared moments, they became more than soldiers. They became fellow humans living out their respective *situations*. It did not mean they stopped being soldiers, but they were not *only* soldiers. Even though they were enemies during war, they still found a way to connect with each other as humans.

Understanding situatedness is a powerful way to unpack how identities are constructed and maintained. It can help us to see how we flatten the story of the other. If I only see someone as liberal or conservative, as a Christian or a Hindu, I miss their texture. What kind of Hindu? How have they changed? Are they kind? In simplifying or assigning to them one story, we miss the opportunity to learn what we do have in common, what they care about, and who can be loved and grieved.

Essentialism

Another dynamic that threatens bridging is *essentialism*. Essentializing is when we think that a certain group has inherent characteristics and that those characteristics are either unchangeable, uniformly experienced, or fixed. Inherent essential traits are seen not as social, but as universal and timeless about a particular group.

Essentialism invites us into a flat understanding of ourselves and the other. We try to explain people by assigning them an essential nature, which means there is no possibility of change. If I can explain women as *essentially* more emotional than men, I should not expect anything else. This logic was used for centuries to restrict women from public life and positions of power. Notice, this claim is not that a particular woman is this way, but all women by their *essential* nature.

Once a group is assigned essential categories, the possibility for movement is lost. And there is little interest in trying to understand the group, or members of it, in ways that would conflict with those essential traits. When I moved from Minneapolis to Columbus, Ohio, I was introduced to some prominent Black leaders. One of them told me he had heard about me. He said he was excited to work together even though I was not a real African American. I asked him why I was not a real African American. He responded that he had heard I was vegetarian and did not eat chicken. Since all real African Americans eat chicken, vegetarians therefore could not be real African Americans.

There may be something special about our social identity, but it is not genetic, fixed, or in our blood. Claims of essentialism deny the importance of our situatedness and our unique spirits. We are certainly impacted by our experiences, but we are not determined by them. Discussion of innate qualities of being African, European, or Indian is just wrong.

We seem to claim that race and ethnic identities are socially constructed and at the same time are also an essential part of our identity. I am concerned that many today are heading toward a kind of racial or ethnic essentialism and also that many are organizing around a kind of colorblind individualism.

Both positions are indeed blind, not to race or ethnicity, but to our situatedness. In terms of the focus on this book, neither of these positions supports bridging. These approaches stop me from bridging with the other—and, moreover, they stop me from seeing the other. They erase curiosity, because the other is already assumed to be known through presumed fixed, essential characteristics.

When a person has been reduced to an essential, there is little else to draw on and much that is missed. Seeing a person as fixed limits curiosity not only about that person or group but about oneself.

My would-be friend in Columbus was not interested in why I was a vegetarian. He knew all he needed to know—that I was not a real African American.

Bridging requires the ability to open up not just to the other but to ourselves. The required vulnerability of bridging is one of the reasons that some will be reluctant to try it. If group X is or does only Y, there is no possibility of movement.

When I was much younger, I went to a party and met a nice woman. We danced and shared stories. As the party came to an end, she asked if we should exchange phone numbers. For some reason she mentioned her political party affiliation, sharing that she knew it was different from mine, but that point did not matter to her. What I responded was: "Well, it matters to me." I declined to exchange numbers. I did not inquire about her position, let alone what her values were or what her story was. What I was doing was flattening her to a single identity—her political party. I pegged her as other, and my interest shrank. And I told a story to myself about what that identity signaled about her that may or may not have been true. Operating from a simple and comfortable frame, I was not interested.

I am not proud of this exchange, and I would like to think I would behave differently today. I am not suggesting I could always bridge, but I can commit to being more willing to engage, willing to be more curious, and even willing to struggle with my differences with another.

In her book *Hospicing Modernity*, scholar and educator Vanessa Machado de Oliveira describes the idea of "many selves" using the metaphor of a bus: each of us has a busload of passengers and a bus driver inside of us. We are not always aware of one another from our seats on the bus, and each of us has different needs and concerns. We have processes and perspectives interacting with other processes and perspectives both inside and outside of the bus.

This metaphor is similar to an African metaphor that we are made up of a committee of selves. When we interact with the world, the appropriate self is sent forth to engage. These metaphors challenge the notion that we are a single and unitary self, something that is closely associated with essentialism. They all suggest that the self has a multifaceted nature and that we don't have complete access to ourselves.

While supporting these insights—and recognizing they might appear strange to many of us—I would also go further. We are not just made up of discrete parts that are called forth, but the parts themselves are processes that are interacting with each other and the world. This paradigm invites a great deal of curiosity and possibility for change and bridging. But essentialism would reject this view of the selves we contain and the change and uncertainty that model entails.

These insights are important as we consider bridging. The failure to see complexity in people limits our curiosity about them. The same is true as we look at ourselves. When we insist on a single and timeless story about ourselves, it limits our ability to see our own multiplicity and possibilities. If we were truly stuck with a single identity, the possibility for changing either ourselves or others would be extremely limited. It could lead us to discussions of purity and to look for expressions of essential traits.

These flat, essentialized stories contrast with the rich, layered, and evolving story we are exploring in this book. Much of the attack on identity politics is an attack on essentialism: the critique is that groups are using ascribed identities as static and innate. The perspective is also closely associated with broad generalizing and stereotypes. Identity politics are also assumed to be concerned only with issues associated with the salient identity of a given group. Under this assumption, groups identified with race are assumed not likely to care about other concerns, such as gay rights or environmental issues.

With this narrow focus, bridging and cross-coalition work would be all but impossible. There are a number of serious flaws in thinking in this way. First, implicitly, and sometimes explicitly, the suggested solution is to drop the importance of identity and focus on a "real" issue, like the economy. But these claims conflate. The suggestion of focusing on "universal" issues easily slips into an unhelpful colorblindness.

We should be concerned when groups organize around a salient identity feature in an exclusive, essential, or breaking manner. But it is not the identity that is so much the problem as the breaking. And the solution that is often offered is also breaking.

Second, there is a failure to appreciate Amartya Sen's insight, mentioned in chapter 5, about how important a characteristic becomes when it is used to threaten someone. When a group is marginalized *because* of their identity, it is more than unreasonable to insist they give up focusing on that identity when that same identity is what is used to justify their second-class participation. This does not mean, though, that we should accept *essential* claims about marginal groups, even when they themselves adopt such claims. If we are to bridge, we may benefit from understanding that a lot of identity politics are really fights about groups and resources.

Reflect

- What are some of the necessary elements that need to be in place for bridging to happen? Make a list.

- What does it mean to turn toward one another instead of turning away? Can you think of an example in your own life where you have turned or could turn toward someone/ some group instead of turning away?

- What is an example of a bridge you're considering in your own life or organization? What is the other's story? What is their story of you? What is your story about yourself/selves?

- How would the changes you're proposing impact the person or group you're bridging with? How would they impact you or your group?

- How quickly are you proposing change? How will that timing feel to you? To the person or group you're bridging with?

- What complexity should you be aware of within the other person or group? Within yourself/selves?

- What sacred symbols should you be aware of and acknowledge? Might you experience conflict between your sacred symbols?

- How are you situated? How is the person or group you're trying to bridge with situated? What dynamics related to race, gender, sexuality, ability, political affiliation, or other characteristics should you be aware of?

8

Short and Long Bridges

I have a friend, Pastor Michael McBride, an activist, minister, and community leader. His faith is important to him and is deeply intertwined with his work in activism. I've worked with Michael for several years and on many things. When I described the concept of bridging to Michael, he took some time to ponder it. He then asked, "But john, are you saying I should bridge with the devil?"

My reply to Michael was, "Don't start with the devil" (and that we should be very careful whom we label as the devil, something I'll return to later). In a similar vein I would say: Don't start bridging with whoever is at the furthest reach of your imagination. Start with someone closer. Start with a short bridge.

Understanding and being able to decipher the possibility and potential of both short and long bridges helps us refine our practice of bridging.

Short Bridges

A *short bridge* is a bridge where the parties in the groups already share a good deal. They may be friends or family. They may belong to the same religious institution or same political party. In many respects, they speak the same language and share many of the same values or outlook on life. Still, there are disagreements. To an observer, these disagreements might seem petty or not even worthy of being called disagreements. If there is a need for a bridge, it seems to be short. And yet even short bridges can be very difficult to build and, if not handled well, can end up breaking otherwise healthy relationships.

What might be considered a short bridge by outsiders is not necessarily short to the groups or individuals involved. Some people might be surprised to find out there are many different sects of Muslims, Christians, Jews, and Hindus. What might be even more surprising is that there can be not only conflict but breaking between these various groups: Christians against other Christians, for example, or Muslims against other Muslims.

At times these breaks can seem intractable. Think of the Troubles in Northern Ireland between the Catholics and the Protestants or the long struggle between Sunni and Shia Muslims in the Middle East. Whose side would Jesus or Muhammad be on? While these groups have a great deal in common, there is enough that is perceived as difference to cause prolonged conflicts full of violence.

My point is not about the particulars of any of the conflicts themselves, but that what in some circumstances might be considered a small difference—something that one might think would require just a short bridge—in fact can need more of a long bridge in practice. Many times, groups with much in common may agree on important goals or an end destination but strongly disagree on the method or strategy for getting there. At times the familiarity itself can add to the intensity of a break. Family members or good friends know how to hurt one another in ways not so available to a stranger. Maybe we should not be surprised that in the United States, the Civil War still stands out of all US conflicts as the deadliest in terms of loss of American lives.

Another example could prove instructive. People might be aware that Hitler was elected to office in Germany through a parliamentary system in which, if a group gets 40 percent of the vote, they will get 40 percent of the seats in the legislature. The head of the government— prime minister or president—is selected by the legislature instead of directly by the people. Such systems are often cited as less likely to produce hard breaking than, say, the American two-party system of winner takes all.

Although the experience in Nazi Germany might give reason for pause, it is clear that parliamentary systems generally create more favorable conditions for compromise. In Germany in 1931, there was not a single majority after the popular vote, which meant a need for possible compromise among parties in order to form a government. Two groups that could have worked together and stopped Hitler were the communists and the socialists.

Would such a compromise have been a long or a short bridge? Most people not familiar with these particular party dynamics might assume this would have been a very short bridge. In practice, though, their differences were experienced as a long bridge—one that was, ultimately, too long to travel. The two groups refused to work with each other and thereby allowed Hitler and his party to form an elected government.

This lesson may seem like it belongs to a far different place and time. Or maybe not. But anyone working in political spaces will not be surprised that there is frequently breaking between groups that seem like they are on the same side.

Given the existence of common ground and even shared goals, why are short bridges so difficult? There are many reasons, but for now I will highlight only a few. Looking at my relationship with my family when I was eleven reveals some examples. You are especially vulnerable to differences and breaks among those who are important to you. It is not just that they know you; they have often played an important role in helping constitute who you are. To put it differently, they have been part of your belonging group. Many of us know of a married couple whose relationship went from one of soft breaking to hard breaking—for example, my two friends discussed in the previous chapter. In much of her work, the author and sociologist Brené Brown writes about belonging, family, and the unique pain experienced when things go awry in our family domains.

Those who are close to us know how to push our buttons. We may feel betrayed and injured by their actions in a way that we would not were they the actions of a stranger. Our guard is down, and we are vulnerable in a way that we are not with strangers. Family and friends can deliver a special kind of hurt.

But there is often a silver lining. Precisely because of our closeness to those where the bridge is short, our antipathy toward them is often complicated, and our space to bridge may be more enduring. We can exact a special pain on those we love. Their need to belong is often most acute in those relationships. So even if there is a break, there is also likely be a residual desire to heal and bridge. In addition, there may be more material, such as community, to help build a bridge.

In my own family, the break that happened was never complete. My parents continued to love me. In some important ways, I continued to be their son and part of the family. My parents and especially my mother over the years were able to trade on this. She never gave up on repairing if not rebuilding the short bridge. She never lost touch with the love of her baby boy. While not all short bridges have access to love and longevity, and even those that do may not be able to use them, long bridges are less likely to have this resource available at all.

Long Bridges

So if short bridges can be so difficult, is there any hope for *long bridges*? For my friend Michael, the implied meaning about bridging with the devil was clear—the long bridge doesn't feel possible to either build or cross.

Who in our own story and imagination is the person or group that threatens our very existence? The other in that story is at the opposite end of a long bridge from us. People usually have little trouble identifying who represents the other on the opposite side of the long bridge. It is the devil. Or maybe the Trump supporter if I am voting Democrat or the Democrat if I am for Trump.

Unless the person or group on the other side of the long bridge is a family member or someone with whom I have already had close contact, I am likely to know of them only as the devil—the worst details of their lives—a lens that sheds very little information or nuance. The details we can make out at this distance are not likely to be endearing or attractive. The devil is one-dimensional in ways that matter. Or so we think.

It's important to note that long bridges more likely come into play at the group level or higher, such as state or international levels, and not at the individual level. In our minds we put Donald Trump and Bernie Sanders supporters into political groups where we may not know or care about the individual desires of individual voters, but instead their collective ones. *They* are likely to represent the antithesis of all the things the opposing group wants and of all the things that the other thinks are good for the collective—in this case, our country. That is one of the reasons we can more easily imagine them as simply evil rather than consider them as complicated people with some agreements and disagreements among them. If the conditions of shared values, language, and symbols are present in the case of short bridges, it is often assumed by both the parties involved that those are not present in long bridges. Do you know or respect my sacred symbols? One might assume that a rural, white, evangelical Trump supporter has nothing in common with an urban, Asian, trans Bernie supporter. And yet this assumption would be wrong. Saying people and groups have common ground does not indicate that bridging can or will happen. But it does open up the possibility.

In the case of short bridges, the parties often agree on the end goals, but they are likely to disagree on the strategy and method to achieve this shared goal. The social scientist Scott E. Page, in his book *The Diversity Bonus*, raises the findings that when there is diversity and there is agreement on shared goals, then diversity can be not only okay but positive. But when there is diversity and there is no agreement on shared goals, diversity is likely to be polarizing and problematic.

Another way of saying this is that where the bridges are experienced as long, there are many more challenges, or at least different ones, to building those bridges.

Let's look at the conditions of long bridges more carefully. The first thing to notice is that a long bridge is not always what it appears to be. Or, as in my discussion with Pastor McBride, can we be sure that the person way on the other side is indeed the devil? If we are willing to seriously entertain this question, we will be calling one of the basic assumptions associated with long bridges into question. Maybe there are no devils, and maybe there are no long bridges.

If it were only that simple. It is not so much that I want to engage with the effort to prove or disprove the existence of a devil; the important point is how we act around those beliefs. Many times, the devil is the other, devoid of redeeming human traits, and bridging is not only not possible but not desirable.

Thinking back to the studies done by Susan Fiske, research has shown that when we deeply other people, they can cease to show up even as human in our subconscious and sometimes even in our conscious. The part of the brain that lights up when we see another human does not light up when groups are deeply othered. Instead, the part of the brain that may light up is associated with disgust.

One can also other by seeing someone as powerful and evil or lowly and of no value. In either case, one is unlikely to imagine it possible or desirable to bridge with such a person or group. They are seen as a threat not just to what I have or want but to my very existence.

Long bridging at the group level is quite different than at the individual level. If one is part of a group that shares a belief in another group's inhumanity and even their evil, that shared belief is likely doing some work to give shape and meaning to the in-group. If your community believes that all evangelical Americans are racist, then trying to bridge with such groups may call your standing in the community into question.

To put it differently, one of the roles of breaking is to give meaning and purpose to one's *own* group. As I mentioned earlier, we other in order to belong. In such a situation, if we stop othering or breaking, then our status in our belonging group may be called into question.

There is an extremely high cost to bridge to a group that one has some negative feelings about. It is not surprising that most people may not be willing to pay this price.

Despite this challenge, hopeful interventions exist. Many groups that organize around long bridges have a leader or influencer who is important to the group. If that person signals that it is okay to bridge, it opens up more possibility. If the group leader bridges, then the threat of losing one's status as a group member is greatly reduced. This does not mean that bridging will happen, but it moves the process closer. The example of Nelson Mandela comes again to mind. Mandela was not only modeling a potential future of belonging for both white and Black South Africans through the honoring of sacred symbols, but he was also using his leadership position to assume a great deal of the risk of building a long bridge.

Similarly, if the person is in other important groups where they experience belonging that is not threatened by bridging, the possibility for bridging is enhanced if the conditions or situatedness is supportive. Removing threats and offering positive incentives can help in the process. Whether to bridge or not is often about safety. There are many benefits to bridging, but there are also risks. To limit or remove the risks can increase the likelihood of bridging. Recall that one of the major motivations for othering and breaking is to belong.

While this is something we all can participate in and sometimes do, leaders and influencers play an oversized role. Think of what has been referred to as "cancel culture." Currently, as many people are trying to figure out how to think and talk about their feelings about the war in Gaza, there is a heightened awareness that saying the wrong thing, or even nothing at all, can have serious consequences impacting where you belong.

Competition

One dynamic that can make both short and long bridging challenging is when the other group is seen to be in competition with our group.

Competition is a particular kind of threat. When competition is present, there is almost always a zero-sum assumption—and at times an explicitly stated story—that if one group wins, the other group must lose. That can make bridging very difficult. These stories might be that a group's life and success are hurting mine—that they are taking our jobs and our resources and there aren't enough of either to go around. Or the stories might be that policies or practices that offer care to another group mean that there is no care left for me. The loss can be seen as happening on various levels including the material, but also the ontological, the spiritual, or the level of status. If a man thinks women need to be submissive to him in order for him to fully express his manhood, he sees her claim for equality and independence to be the cause of breaking, not his beliefs.

As I shared in the story of my family, in the church I was raised in until I left it at eleven, we were taught that a man was supposed to be the head of the family. But in my own family this was not practiced straightforwardly. My family was in many ways matrilineal. So being embedded in the church made for an interesting dynamic. I had conversations with male and female members of the family about the ordained role of the man to lead while the family practice was very different.

The conditions in the family are often a complicated mixture of care and status, and that mixture may be asymmetrical. The female, for example, may lose out in external status, but within the family she may benefit. The assumption is that if the father or other males do well, the women will in some measure share in the benefits. The family, even when hierarchically organized, may be tempered with care.

Let's consider more challenging examples, since those are more often the ones we have to grapple with. There is a long history of working-class Black Americans being seen as competition to working-class white Americans. But this perception of a competition of equals has not played out in symmetrical ways. Black workers were systematically kept out of unions and labeled as being antiunion and strikebreakers. Not being able to participate in unions meant that the causes of Black workers were not championed to management and that Black workers received lower wages and fewer benefits, as outlined in David Roediger's *The Wages of Whiteness*. This practice not only created a dual labor market, it also created a racialized concept of the labor market that we continue to live with today. This speaks to an underlying story that white people have an inherent deservedness over Black people. We can recall Ronald Reagan's comment about reserving sympathy for "deserving" rather than "undeserving" poor. This narrative is still alive today, as the phrase "working class" too often means advocating for support for the white working class while excluding the working class people of color. With this narrative comes a belief about which class deserves respect, dignity, and concern, and which may not.

Even when people from different groups are operating in the same space, there is still too often a story of competition. Among many activist groups, the story is that advancing people of color may mean limiting the material and psychological status of white people. For many conservatives, white people can do well only if they maintain their place of status and dominance. But there is another story, one where white people and people of color *all* do well; in fact, they do well in part because the other group is doing well. Before we think of dividing the pie, it might be useful to think about both redefining and in some cases enlarging the pie.

In these competitions is embedded a story told in zero-sum terms and based on a narrative of scarcity. Underlying these claims of material scarcity is something much more nuanced. Activists who organize primarily around a material and class model are often puzzled over why it can be so difficult to get low-income whites to make common cause with low-income people of color. The thinking is that when they make common cause, both groups benefit. Sometimes this condition is lamentably described as poor whites acting against their self-interest. The limitation of this story is the assumption that our material interests are the same as our self-interest. Groups are often competing not only for material but for status.

We see a similar competition-and-dominance framing when we look how the US relationship with China is addressed and discussed. In its reporting on anything to do with China, the *New York Times*, the American paper of record and one that many consider a fair paper, often puts forth an implied narrative that the central problem underlying global politics and economics is China's threat to US dominance in the world. Discussions are framed in a such a way as to suggest US dominance is natural and appropriate and that not only will China challenge this dominance, but it might come to dominate the US itself, which is unnatural and undesirable.

Two obvious elements are missing from this narrative. One is discussion of the appropriateness of anyone dominating. The second is the inability to imagine any country existing *without* dominance. This example is not indirectly signaling support for China or its policies; it's a direct challenge to the zero-sum narrative about competition and a challenge to a foundational narrative of natural dominance.

Of course, I know some will simply assert that a nondominant position is not real or even natural.

We see a similar zero-sum narrative when we look at contemporary US elections and political parties. We are witnessing a growing assertion of white supremacy and the call for white control. The Department of Homeland Security found that white supremacy was the number one domestic terrorist threat in the country. Those who embrace supremacy and dominance find the call for equality unnatural and a threat. The Republican Party alignment has become deeply factionalized, which in many ways plays out along racial lines as well. White conservative Christians are overwhelmingly Republican, and the Republican ideology has become not just tacitly but largely openly anti–people of color, antitrans, anti-Muslim, and just plain anti-.

So much so that few Republicans have been willing to challenge Florida Governor Ron DeSantis on his attacks on diversity, including his administration's claim that slavery may have even benefited Black Americans. While this type of racialized narrative was rejected by most Republicans as recently as 2016, such othering has now become part of the price of belonging to the Republican mainstream.

There are, of course, fair people across the political spectrum who object to this type of othering, but they have largely been silenced, or they silence themselves to maintain their group status. The core of the current Republican Party as expressed through Trumpism is deep breaking anchored in the weaponizing of fear of the other. For example, Governor DeSantis bragged that he supports using deadly force against immigrants suspected of bringing drugs into the United States.

And while Republicans and Democrats seem to be in a zero-sum competitive story, they can all agree on China and the threat of TikTok.

When I assert that we must promote a world where all belong and none are othered, I am asked, "What about Trump? Is he in our circle of human concern?" The answer is emphatically yes. One might also be asking, "Isn't naming Trump and the Republican Party as engaging in acts of othering itself a form of othering and breaking?" While such a question could be reasonable, I believe the answer is no.

Including someone in our circle of human concern does not mean that we cannot point out when they are engaging in othering, especially when they have the power of the state controls. Political decisions shape our quality of life.

Today, there is evidence to suggest that we Americans are as polarized as we have ever been since the Civil War. According to the Listen First Project, 61 percent of Americans say they are concerned that the US could be on the verge of another Civil War, even as 79 percent say they would be willing to play a part in reducing social division in America if given the opportunity. It is not the Republican Party that I am focusing on but the deeply breaking and othering position that has become the norm. One only has to go back to 2015 and '16 to find many mainstream Republicans who warned against such breaking and othering. They either have been largely pushed out of the party or have adopted the toxic approach themselves. Another example of this radical shift of position is how many Republican leaders initially condemned the January 6, 2021, violent attack on the United States Capitol Building and then later moved to defend the January 6 insurrection as patriotic, as this position appeared to be a requirement to participate in mainstream Republican politics.

Statistics show us that the majority of Americans long for belonging. We must not normalize seeing our political opponents as enemies who must be defeated at all costs when they are opposed to belonging.

And naming those who are involved in such deep breaking and othering is not the same as refusing to acknowledge their humanity. The danger of the fragmentation happening today is that we can easily become willing to deny not only the other's humanity and dignity but even their right to exist.

Do our politics have to rely on demonizing others? Should our concern with the current dysfunction in our politics have to destroy the goodwill of our society? Is the dehumanizing of our fellow Americans something we should accept?

The answer is no. We often assume that bridging and belonging require a neutral posture that is largely value free. But this assumption is off. Belonging *is* a value. Belonging puts a value on human life and more. And that value is equality and dignity.

Positions that would deny this foundational value must be challenged, but without denying the humanity of the person with counter views. The process of bridging and working toward belonging includes some guardrails. They can be questioned, but in doing so we are likely to come up with the same or new ones. We are not likely to come to a neutral or value-free position. I was asked if I would go to rural Minnesota and speak to some right-wing white Trump supporters. My response was that I would, but there needed to be guardrails in place, including a rule of no violence.

After the murder of George Floyd in 2020, I was asked to help convene a meeting with a well-known former state Supreme Court justice and several activist groups. I stated I would, but only if there were some clear guardrails. One of them was that the justice would not be verbally attacked. The groups did not agree, and the meeting did not take place.

What are the conditions necessary for a bridging conversation to take place? These guardrails are important and must be worked on. At the same time, we must be careful not to put forth too many conditions to avoid having the engagement. Earlier we talked about how extreme inequality undermines bridging, but with a caution: we do not need absolute equality before engagement.

Similarly, concerns about safety often arise, but complete safety is not possible or even desirable in some cases. Bridging does involve risk. Engaging with others involves some risk, but so does not engaging. One must consider what guardrails are needed while making an effort to engage.

I have previously suggested that the concern with fragmentation and factions was present from the beginning of the existence of the US as a country. The Federalist Papers, which were important in supporting the ratification of the US Constitution, paid considerable attention to addressing factionalism and extreme concentration of power. The papers took into account such issues as the situatedness of large and small states, as well as rural versus urban areas and, of course, slave versus free states. Even before "we as a nation" was conceived, theorists deeply contemplated different stories about how to create a society where people could flourish. Thomas Jefferson conceived a nation where all men would be equal. But to paraphrase Chief Justice Roger Taney when confronted, in the infamous *Dred Scott* case in 1857, with the protection afforded people under the Constitution, Taney insisted Blacks were not people and could never belong in the political community of the United States. Rather, they were enslaved or free; being in a free state did not, for Taney, change their lack of the right to citizenship.

By 2045, changing US demographics are projected to result in the white population becoming the minority for the first time since the founding of the nation. This loss of status among whites is coupled with decreasing economic opportunity as well as instability among all groups.

Of course, it is more than a small step to assume that if white people are no longer the racial majority, this would entail a shift in the power and prestige of whiteness. And is there really such cohesiveness in whiteness? What if the category of whiteness expands to include more than just European identification? Maybe more importantly, why would we buy into the breaking story that an increase in the number of nonwhites necessarily means a threat to whites?

Part of this goes back to the issue of domination. Whiteness as an ideology included both status over nonwhites as well as the right and even responsibility to dominate the racial and gender other. If one buys into the mindset that one is either dominant or subordinate, then the loss of domination by one's group means that the group will become subordinate.

In a sense, we have a problem imagining a world of equals. If one's identity is tied up with dominance, then the loss of dominance is also an attack on one's identity. Not all people who are considered white embrace this approach, but a growing number do. And while I am talking about an ideology, often material arrangements reflect this. The idea of the wages of whiteness, to use David Roediger's phrase, is not just symbolic.

These concerns about whiteness and power have been with us for decades and are still very present. Consider, for example, the role of whites-only primary elections that existed in this country until the 1960s. Voting is an important right that promotes participation and belonging. Many Republican voting reforms in recent years are clearly aimed at limiting the voting and participation of nonwhites. There is now a new push to create a smaller, ethnic we and exclude again the racial, ethnic other. This shows up also in the broad attacks on DEI.

The need for white purity and dominance creates a constant, supercharged state of fear of the radical other. We are not far removed from the segregationist concerns of the 1950s. It is important to stress that I am talking about the ideology of whiteness, not people who are phenotypically white. Currently California, Hawaii, New Mexico, and Texas all have nonwhite majorities. Is there an indication that whites are being dominated in these states?

Whatever the facts are, they will not necessarily influence the stories we believe or the policies we adopt due to those beliefs.

A manufactured scarcity exists that promotes breaking between groups. In California, where I teach university students, there have been long-standing fights about affirmative action in higher education. We have an increasing number of bright and highly motivated students who want to go to our state's public universities. But we haven't created enough space to meet the demand of so many bright students. Questions then arise about whether we should let in more Black students, or more Native students, or more Latinx students. And if we do, what does that mean for white or Asian American students? People sue the university using the frame that their child didn't get in because people of color used affirmative action to take the available spots. After several attempts to roll back affirmative action with a white plaintiff, the conservative legal activist Edward Blum, founder of Students for Fair Admissions, moved to an alternative—the Asian American student. In the context of education, Asian Americans have often been cast as the model minority and white adjacent. That strategy fulfilled Blum's goal in 2023 when the US Supreme Court effectively struck down race-based affirmative action admissions to colleges in *Students for Fair Admissions v. Harvard*. But we must be careful not to overly categorize. All groups—whites, Asian Americans, Blacks, Latinos, and Native Americans—are diverse; we are not just talking about people but stories and ideologies.

I would ask: Why the suits against affirmative action? We could instead be suing to build more universities. Our point of origin should be that we can never have too many bright students, not which students get the limited spots. The whole debate is framed incorrectly. Once we are in an *us versus them* zero-sum struggle, we are well on our way to breaking and othering. Scarcity thinking often happens in a narrow frame and with limited context. For example, there's no scarcity of prisons in California, and yet our ire and energy are directed against bright students. To put this in a larger context, we have a court that reflects former President Donald Trump and a party that sees a broad attack on Black people and others as a way to construct belonging for right-wing white people.

Three Types of Bridging

I see bridging practices as sitting on a continuum, with three points along it being transactional, transformational, and spiritual bridging. While no neat divide exists between these three points, it is useful to understand how they are different. I will discuss the first two points below and devote the final chapter of the book to spiritual bridging.

Transactional Bridging

Transactional bridging is generally driven by a desire to produce a particular result in the other person. Some of the important increase in a focus on bridging has come from the community organizing and civic engagement space. I have worked closely with a number of these groups. The bridging they engage in is most likely to be transactional. In this space, the effort is usually geared toward winning something. Persuasion is happening: I am talking and listening to the other person with the hope I will convince them to do something to support my side, often to vote a certain way on a certain issue or person. My listening to you has a very clear motive. This type of work is often described in terms of building power or just simply winning.

Some may question if this should even be called bridging. Isn't there a deep contradiction? If I am listening to you only to change you or get you on my side, is that really bridging? Despite this understandable tension, I do think this kind of transactional exchange is bridging. Whatever the reasons we decide to bridge, we should be relatively transparent with ourselves and with the person we are engaging with. One may be willing to listen and be clear that they have a willingness to listen. One can think of listening just to prove the other person wrong, or one could listen to get a deeper understanding of the other while offering little or no openness to change. *Transaction* suggests doing something to get something. But one can also think of *transaction* as exchange and compromise: one is willing to trade. These exchanges or compromises are not based on a new understanding of the other side but on a cost-benefit analysis that shows there is benefit in connecting and bridging.

Though I do have a concern that bridging might devolve into a technique used just to win, the reality is that, conceptually and logically, things are rarely pure in the messy world we live in. While instrumental and noninstrumental action—doing something because it gets you something else versus doing something because it has value in itself—may seem like polar opposites, the fact is that in life they often coexist.

There is a sense in transactional bridging that I am interested in you only because you will help me get what I want. But maybe in the process, I will help you get something you want as well. As long as we are straightforward, there is nothing wrong with such a transaction. Robert Putnam describes similar processes as *specific reciprocity*: I give you something in exchange for what you give me.

I was discussing this tension and even contradiction with a good friend and great organizer. In politics we want to win. We may even feel we have to win. So we want a very specific outcome. The very push for an outcome risks turns bridging into a transaction. But as my friend noted, people will quickly notice when you are not really interested them but just want their vote.

What I have seen happen in transactional bridging is more subtle. The very process of listening and being present appears to be much more effective at getting someone to open up to a different perspective. And as we practice deeper listening, not only might the person open up on an issue, but they will usually open up as a human being.

So here is the contradiction: The more deeply and authentically we can be present with the other, the more likely there will be movement.

But the very effort toward movement can make us less authentic and thereby limit movement.

When we really listen, not only is the person we are engaging with likely to change, so are we. The practice of deep listening, even if used only as a technique at first, can cause us to move into real listening, with the possibility of transforming both us and the other. By running the risk of vulnerability, we might blur the lines from *us and them* to *us and us*, even if just for a moment.

The good news is that more and more groups are embracing the need to bridge. While bridging in some form has always been around, even if it wasn't called that, we are seeing an explicit call for bridging and an exponential increase in the number of groups that are promoting bridging of various kinds. If one had searched for groups doing work under the label of bridging even five years ago, one would have found numbers in the single digits. Today, there are hundreds of groups actively doing this work and specifically naming it as bridging. Many of these groups may have started out engaged in transactional bridging, but as the work deepened, they have begun to move into more transformational bridging.

Transformational Bridging

While transactional bridging often navigates within existing arrangements without its participants imagining new possibilities, *transformational bridging* adds to the mix of what's possible in the arrangements themselves. When we're doing something transformational, we are often calling to go beyond the existing status quo.

Many more options are on the table in this type of bridging. When a transformational action turns to people, it is much more relational than transactional bridging, and the results are more open and fluid. In the political realm, consider if someone was interested in voting for a Republican or a Democrat; a transactional effort for one party to win might mean garnering the required number of votes for the electoral college. But a transformational effort might add an entirely different way of expressing one's preference. Transformational action might call for the end of the electoral college in favor of a parliamentarian arrangement.

Another example is to consider the approach to nation-statehood in Europe following World War I. A central question was how to divide power among the various nations that had been involved in the war. This was largely a transactional agreement that tweaked existing arrangements.

Thirty years later, following World War II in Europe, the negotiating parties moved toward the formulation of a European Union, a scenario with a different set of relationships and mode of power sharing. The nature of these arrangements affected our interests and wrought transformational change. There was not just a question of what the nations and people who were part of the existing system should do, but a need to rethink the old systems themselves.

Transactional and transformational bridging shape not only institutions differently but also the people within them. Transactional change assumes the arrangements will not change and also that people within them will not—that there are fixed interests, needs, and desires. Transformational bridging more easily leans into shifting relationships and new containers. Bridging with a tilt toward the transformational calls for more imagination and vulnerability. Beyond the question of what we want or what we should do, it can raise the question of who we are.

Transformational bridging can occasionally slip into magical thinking. The call for radical, transformational, systemic, and structural change can lose sight of the humans it is meant to help.

When done well, transactional and transformational bridging can be aligned. It is not always easy to identify when something is transactional and something is transformational. Sometimes small changes end up having large impact, and sometimes what appears monumental turns out to be of little importance. Although we have talked about bridging and breaking and othering and belonging as distinct—because they are, and breaking them each down helps us to grasp how they work—the reality is that aspects of these dynamics can be present together. You may bridge at one point only to break at another. You might also identify some aspect that serves as connection even in the midst of breaking.

Academic and activist Loretta Ross gives us another way of thinking about long and short bridges by looking at what percentage of things we agree on—90, 75, 50, and 0. The idea is that we might agree on 90 percent of what is important and disagree on 10 percent (or 75 and 25). Her point is that we should not get stuck on the 10 or even 25 percent disagreement while ignoring all the places where we agree.

And yet even when we agree on goals and values, we may disagree on how to get there—the theory of change. A difference is not necessarily considered small because it is small. It is considered small because we decide to treat it as small. Even if we disagree with someone or think they are wrong (and often matters are not so clear as right and wrong), can we afford them the graciousness to still belong? Such a question is highly dependent on the context of us, them, and the circumstances. When breaking becomes systematic, there is little room for grace.

I believe in the promise of proliferative change. While the increasing number of groups interested in bridging is an encouraging sign, there is some indication that one of the reasons for this growth is concern over the even faster expansion of breaking and fragmentation. We should work toward bridging and belonging as a norm, not only in the US but all over the world. We can elevate and share examples of bridging daily, where our cooperation and care for each other is the norm.

Reflect

- Can you imagine a person or situation in your life (past or present) that might be met with a short bridge? What is the end goal? What points of similarity are present? What points of difference?

- Can you imagine a person or situation in your life (past or present) that might be met with a long bridge? What is the end goal? What points of similarity are present? What points of difference? What leaders might help support the bridging?

- What is at risk when you attempt to bridge?

- What guardrails, or measures of safety and protection, would need to be in place for you to imagine bridging, either long or short?

- What are your goals in bridging—do you hope the bridging will be transactional, transformational, or spiritual?

9

Bridging and Spirituality

A t its deepest expression, I believe bridging is a spiritual project. To me, spirit is where we show up in the world a certain way because that's who we believe we are called to be by life itself, of which we are already a part.

Spirit is about connection and openness, where that openness is an orientation, an openness to life in its myriad expressions. Not just openness to what we want or even what we think. Those are preferences, not openness.

When there is radical openness, it is not simply that "I am open" but that the opening goes beyond the I. We often have the sense that the I is the one acting on the world. This is the basis for much of what is called modern thought—that the world is there to be observed and acted on by me, or the I, as the self.

But a different orientation exists: that the I is a linked part of the world, and as the world changes, so does the I. In this perspective we are radically interrelated to and with the world. When we act on the world, the world necessarily acts on us. This cocreation, then, is a process wherein we and the world are forever engaged. It is what the great Vietnamese monk and peace activist Thich Nhat Hahn referred to as *interbeing*. This sensibility is also captured by much of the work of the Buddhist author and environmental activist Joanna Macy.

Recognizing Our Shared
Humanity and Suffering

We are most likely to be confronted with bridging when there is fear or pain. Often, we are thinking of some separation between us and another. Bridging is about healing the tear of separation. My father would say it is the separation itself that is the injury, and our work is to both live our connection to each other and to heal that pain. Buddhists would say that separation is an illusion, albeit a very painful one.

Some insist bridging can only occur after the illusion and the pain have been addressed. As I've shared several times already, you must decide if and when to engage in bridging. Each party must determine whether they have preconditions that must be met, and what they are, in order to bridge. After considering this, some will choose not to bridge or to only bridge within their own group.

Others may bridge only if they are reasonably sure they will benefit in some concrete way. Whether this is bridging may be questionable, but at any rate it is not what I consider bridging in a spiritual sense. Bridging as a spiritual practice is not a transaction. When we engage in a type of foundational bridging, we are not doing so because the other person is then going to do something for us or because we're going to get something from them.

When we approach a person with vulnerability and openness, it doesn't necessarily mean that they'll agree with us. It doesn't mean we'll end up liking them. When we show up willing to bridge, what it does mean is that we recognize their inherent humanity, and nothing can take that away—neither their actions nor their beliefs. It means we are willing to sit with their humanity in its messiness, not expecting purity.

But what if the *other* we're willing to bridge with does not recognize our humanity? While this may be a reasonable place to draw a line in other types of bridging, it is not the line when we are bridging from a spiritual space. In spiritual bridging, there is no line.

The connectedness of the world is not dependent on our recognizing it. Certainly there are serious and at times possibly dire consequences when we fail to recognize our shared humanity, and yet even amid tragic conditions, we remain connected.

As I have mentioned, I am more than a little skeptical of purity. Yes, I would like the other person to recognize my humanity. But even if they do not—and they may not—bridging means I still try to recognize theirs.

When we engage with another, we are the universal looking out at the universal looking back. That's part of the way that we claim our own humanity, which I see as part of a spiritual practice. We don't have to give up our humanity even if someone insists on othering us and denying our humanity. We are not indifferent or impervious, but neither do we let their animosity define us or them.

Bridging at this deeper level is not about winners or losers. Bridging shows us that it is our responsibility to imagine and cocreate a better future without any guarantee we will succeed. We are not cocreating just for ourselves and our group but for life itself. The very concept of cocreating calls us into a relationship of mutuality, free of domination.

Is it conceivable for there to be an *other* when no possible commonality exists? I think the answer from a belonging perspective is an emphatic no. Can we remain open to the other's situatedness, to their inherent humanity? It may be more impactful to think of someone's situatedness rather than try to understand their personal motivations, if such a thing were even possible. Who is that infinite other that has nothing in common with us? That person does not exist. For starters, we were all born, and we will all die. And we share much more than that.

If you were to take from this that I do not care about circumstances or anyone's profound and mundane suffering, I would quickly reply that nothing could be further from the truth. Belonging and bridging bring us into an even deeper caring and loving relationship with the other, with ourselves, and with life itself.

This is likely to cause its own suffering. I have lost many loved ones—both my parents, two of my brothers, and more friends than I can count. I think of my children, knowing that they will suffer and die. Right now I am thinking of all the children and adults who will die in violent conflicts around the world. I think of all the people who are experiencing surplus suffering, like the unhoused, and all those made to feel like they do not belong, and more. All this makes my heart hurt, because I care. It's because we care that we will suffer. And I care about life and its various expressions a great deal.

But you may ask: "What if I or my group is not concerned with spirituality? Would it then make sense for me to bridge, for instance, to persuade or win?" This question becomes even sharper when we factor in the risk and vulnerability associated with bridging among groups in different contexts and what I referred to as situatedness.

Should you make a cost-benefit analysis or a utilitarian decision to bridge? Obviously, only you can answer such questions for yourself. I have answered the question for me.

The Sense of Self—Separate or Connected?

Instead of engaging in persuasion, I will share how I think about these questions from different perspectives. Remember we started the book by talking about the challenge of rapid change. This refers not just to a change in the world out there, but to a change inside, in who we are. What will it mean to be white, Asian American, or gay in twenty years? It is not clear.

What is clear is that it will mean something different than it does today. Even now, each of these categories is multifaceted, contextual, and unstable. Our ground of being is constantly shifting, but sometimes at a pace that we hardly notice. Part of the anxiety that this change brings is that my group will no longer fit or belong in this changing world. That anxiety becomes all the more poignant if we believe this displacement of belonging is caused by the other.

Some may note that they do not have to wait for an emerging world to feel othered and homeless. This already reflects their daily life.

But what would the self and the group look like in a world where all belonged and none were othered? Where a person's dignity was part of their birthright for being alive? What kind of self would such a reality require? What would our institutional arrangements be in such a world?

We can only vaguely sketch this world, because it must be cocreated with others, and not just with other human life but with all life, including the earth itself.

As I have discussed earlier in the book, much has been written that asserts our interconnectedness. In a spiritual context, that means we are all part of the divine. Yet simply asserting a belief in our connection is not *proof*. Perhaps we would be more convinced by modern science, political research, public health studies, or psychology. Across all these areas there have been many experiments to show the critical nature of belonging for humans and other primates. Is this proof enough? Can anyone actually prove that we are all connected?

You might rather ask if we can instead prove the *contrary*—that is, can we prove that we are *not* connected to one another or to the earth? Breaking and othering are so deeply embedded in our everyday practices at multiple levels—do those dynamics reflect our deepest human nature?

The work I've done in this book is to reject that simplistic claim.

I will make something explicit that I have been hinting at. I have posited that belonging and bridging ask us to recognize that we are interrelated, all part of a profoundly connected ecosystem where each relies on others to live.

I also stated that much of Western civilization is founded on a notion of the separate, autonomous, individual self who exercises free will and independent judgment. Maybe those who take issue with James Baldwin's claim that each of us contains the other are the same ones insisting that we are all separate individuals.

If we believe that belonging is foundational—that is, that our *we* as living beings is constituted through our relationship with others in a tightly interdependent set of social relationships—then it is only in connection that the *I* as an individual properly understood comes alive.

Claims about the self are no small thing. This line of questioning asks: "What is the nature of the self?" Many wonderful books and articles take on this inquiry. On interbeing, a number of Buddhist and other texts assert both that life is profoundly interconnected and that there is no stable, permanent self. I also have little doubt that there are good and maybe even great books that suggest we are all autonomous individuals. As important as these questions are, I will not be able to do them justice in this book.

What is important is why the concept of the self is critical in our discussion of bridging.

One of the main implications I want to focus us on is that a foundational fear of *not belonging* is a disquiet around the possibility that the individual self does not exist. One of the profound insights from Buddhism is not self-realization, but no self-realization. The concept of a stable, permanent self that plays such an important role in Western imagination is only an illusion. We not only know this at some level, but we're also haunted by this lack.

Some expression of this tension about whether we are separate, individual selves shows up across disciplines, from philosophy to biology to physics.

I will restate this position. We long for permanence, but we know at some level that things are impermanent. This means that the self is also impermanent. From the Buddhist perspective, impermanence is not a concept to be debated on the basis of analysis, but a reality that is experienced. The disquiet that is attached to ontological suffering is our effort and failure to grasp onto a sense of permanence, which is a fiction. Instinctively, we are aware of this.

"Okay," you say, "but john, I'm not a Buddhist." Fair enough. Perhaps you may want to look at similar insights about the impermanence and mutability of the self, research that has shown up in the field of neuroscience by such prominent scientists as Robert Sapolsky, who posits that there is no permanent self and that the sovereign self, so often pushed in the Western world, is an unhelpful myth.

Still, there is an urge to be seen as an individual. And at the same time there is an urge to be connected and in relationship. Roberto Unger expresses this as our infinite need for each other *and* our profound fear of each other. Without the *other*, there is no self, but with the *other*, the self may be threatened. Furthermore, he rejects that it is an either/or condition and instead suggests that there is a need to provide space for connection *and* for privacy. He refuses the binary of *individualism versus collectivism* and instead embraces a more nuanced position.

Are we connected, or are we separate? Yes! This is a central tension in modern thought.

The dilemma is captured by a metaphor used by the nineteenth-century German philosopher Arthur Schopenhauer. He likened human relations to porcupines in the cold. They try to gather close together to share their warmth, but in doing so they stick and injure each other. We need each other in ways that require that we be vulnerable to each other. Yet that vulnerability exposes us to risk. The mistake is thinking that we can close off from each other and be safe. Vulnerability exposes us to life itself.

Interconnection or Independence?

This fear of connection and fixation on separation and independence is captured in psychology and philosophy in the archetype of the self-made man or as *causa sui*. The motif shows up often in American culture, from cowboy westerns to the popular science fiction show *Star Trek*. In many of these stories we are presented with a hero who appears to have little need for the others. The hero is most often alone—unmarried or estranged from partner and family. It is not accidental that this hero is usually a he.

In *Star Trek*, the greatest fear is not of death but of being absorbed into the collective being of the Borg. In real life, this fear has led us into a cul-de-sac of isolation, fear, and loneliness. We need each other and can be terrified of that need, or of each other, both at the same time.

In the West, we try to solve this dilemma through a distorted type of independence that spares us from intimacy and vulnerability. This independence does not show up solely in our myths but is deeply reflected in our politics as well. One of the recurringly stated oppositions to helping people in physical need is that we will breed *dependency*. Part of our long hostility toward the poor has been the assumption that if we help them, they will become too dependent on us. We live in false binaries that are based on fear of life. We either stand alone and self-made, or we are absorbed in the mindless collective. This generalized fear becomes supercharged when we are confronted with someone we have designated as *other*. They are coming not just for our jobs but our freedom and our soul.

Many people have taken stories about our supposed independence from the first book of the Bible, Genesis, to an even deeper level. In the biblical story of Cain, he kills his brother, Abel, out of jealousy. God then rhetorically inquires of Cain, "Where is Abel?" Cain famously replies, "Am I my brother's keeper?"

The implied and universal answer from this story is "Yes, we are our brothers' and sisters' keepers."

Yet too many today not only assert they are *not* the keeper of their brothers and sisters, but that we are not even brothers and sisters at all.

When this type of story is imprinted upon the mythology of a culture that is organized around a belief in God, when our inherent connection is denied by fellow citizens, at some level, for believers, it means the connection is denied by the God whom they believe governs society. Recall my expulsion from home and church when I was eleven: it was not only that I was being rejected from those relationships, but at a deeper level I believed I was being rejected by God as well.

When we look at the nature of the ancient African concept of *ubuntu*—meaning "I am because you are"—we see the importance of how our interconnection shows up in non-Western culture. How we see our relationship to one another has consequences. Ubuntu suggests that we need one another, not just to negotiate what we want in life, but for our very being. If this is correct, then without one another or without belonging, our very constitution is called into question. In a group conversation with former justice of the Constitutional Court of South Africa Albie Sachs, he stated that ubuntu and belonging are animating values in their constitution and in the country.

What are the values that animate America or the area where you live?

Seeing One Another's Humanity

Belonging is neither dependency nor independence. The work of Valarie Kaur on revolutionary love calls for us to move to a more direct approach—not independence or dependence, but dependent on being interdependent. Russian geographer and scholar Peter Kropotkin asserts this is our evolutionary heritage—to thrive in our mutuality.

The interconnectedness of our beings is one profound expression of the spiritual aspect of our lives and of life in general. I believe that we are all interconnected, even if we don't honor or live out or even believe in such connections. We may live on a more mundane plane, but I would claim that the mundane itself is also an expression of our connection and spirituality.

For those of you who reject these assertions, and possibly reject the entire idea of spirituality, why might you bridge? I would reiterate, if you are dead set on not bridging, then don't. But even if you decide not to bridge, can you avoid breaking? The purpose of this book is not to convince or persuade but to share.

But maybe you are on the fence and trying to parse this question without a belief in spirituality. Are there other reasons you might bridge, or not? The answer is yes. There indeed is likely a cost or even a risk associated with bridging, but there may be a greater cost associated with not bridging. Perhaps you will embrace transactional bridging but not transformational.

As I discussed earlier, a good friend who is a community organizer has been skeptical of a spiritual justification for bridging. Recently, after several years and many discussions, he decided to experiment with long bridges. This was not just a personal decision. He was committing his organization's resources to engage with people who may have very different goals then he has. When I asked him why he was doing this after years of resisting, his answer was more pragmatic and instrumental than spiritual. He shared that just focusing on short bridges with people who agree on goals was not working. His goal now was not just winning but creating new conditions wherein we can see one another's humanity.

I used to ask this friend: "If you win, what will you do with the losers?" He said he's never had an answer to that question that he found acceptable. He still wants to win, but now he believes that unless we can build a container to have the bridging conversations and see one another's humanity, there is no stable win for any of us.

Others may make a different calculation than my friend's and decide that there are too many risks associated with bridging and not enough upsides. So instead of bridging, and certainly instead of engaging a long bridge, one may possibly decide to bridge only with one's own group and build collective power, to be perhaps the winners instead of the losers.

In responding to this position, let's consider some of the risks often associated with bridging. One is vulnerability. Bridging calls for us to remain open and vulnerable. There is psychological and emotional vulnerability. Psychology now recognizes that emotional and psychological injuries can be just as real and devastating as physical injury. Some of this vulnerability involves engaging the possibility that we too might be changed by the encounter.

Where othering is deliberately engaged in, injuries may indeed occur. To assess the likelihood of such an injury, one must consider the situatedness of the people involved, their environment, and their history. While this is true for everyone, it is especially the case for groups of individuals who are marginalized and/or traumatized. This is one of the reasons each person and each group must make its own assessment of their willingness to bridge. But where these conditions exist, the most constructive response may be to try to create an environment where the threat of injury is reduced to an acceptable level.

This is often hinted at as the need for a safe environment within which to have difficult or vulnerable conversations. While the need to feel safety is understandable and may at times even be necessary, we must be careful not to overcorrect. The goal should be to be *safe enough*, which is not the same as completely safe. Even when one can reduce extreme threats, life and engagement require openness, which necessarily entails some possibility of discomfort and even injury. To try to create complete safety will not only fail but may also produce its own injuries and limit life.

Bridging even at the transactional level will require some degree of faith and grace. Precautions can be taken and at times should be— for example, making the request to avoid personal attacks on anyone present during bridging conversations—and yet complete assurance can never exist.

To open to the possibility of reaching the other person, and of them reaching you, will require us to go beyond hope and employ a degree of trust and faith that the other will reciprocate and treat us with care.

And when we are injured or disappointed in such an encounter, what story can we tell ourselves that will allow us to continue to remain open to bridging again?

In the middle of a deep feeling, it may not seem possible to feel anything else. But that is seldom truly the case. We have all witnessed how young children have an overwhelming emotion, then almost immediately move to a very different state. Is there something about children that we could learn from? Plenty. Children are wonderful models of openness and vulnerability, unafraid to feel big feelings and also to let them move through them.

Not every risk we take will turn out well. We are both deliberately and inadvertently vulnerable. Life on its own terms will bring suffering. We do not have to add what I call surplus suffering to the ontological suffering of life. That we are all vulnerable and all suffer is part of the reason to bridge.

Still, we must each make our own choice about when we will bridge and under what conditions. As I stated, there may be times that it is not right for someone to engage in bridging. There may be a need for guardrails. There will be times and conditions under which one might decide not to bridge. I believe these should be rare and not the default. We must live in the now even in the midst of breaking and pain.

I also maintain that we cannot heal without bridging. Does that mean I am suggesting we bridge *to heal*? And that bridging *precedes* healing?

I am suggesting both.

Healing is not something that happens and then is done. We will be addressing the injury of this illusory separation problem for our entire life. And it is doubtful we can achieve very much if we break in a world that itself is broken.

Embracing the Fullness of Life

While we are likely to be aware of some of the risks of bridging, we too often ignore the risk of *not bridging*. The biblical story of the Good Samaritan again comes to mind.

I assert throughout this book that not only are my belonging and dignity *not* diminished by acknowledging those considered *other*, to the contrary, they are enhanced by recognizing the other.

The fullness of belonging means we don't put off life, love, and joy until we have removed suffering. Joy and suffering can share the same space and certainly the same life.

I would caution against this binary: we do not have to banish fear and anger before we say hello to faith and connection. Vacations and holidays (*holy days*) are necessary, but we don't need to wait for those to experience joy. Joy and love are part of our whole life. And that life will also have pain and suffering, both yours and the world's. To suffer with is to bridge. To suffer with is to experience compassion. I learned early expressions of this from my parents. Their lives had more than a little suffering but also had a bounty of joy and love.

What does it mean to not put off life? A big and maybe unanswerable question. To me it means that life is not always linear. Several things may be happening at once that are informing one another. In the midst of struggle and sadness, there is also joy and love. Making space and acceptance for all of this is part of life and is what I think of as a spiritual practice.

I am aware that it is not enough to share facts or space with each other, but we need to explore meaning as well. I have talked to many people engaged in bridging work, and many feel hopeless and even burned out. There is much pain in the world. As I write this passage, I am feeling the pain in the Middle East. The pain of Jews and Palestinians. But the joy and love of my family and children are in me, too, in the same time and space. Sometimes this makes the pain of suffering with others even more acute.

When we are in deep pain, that pain can be both debilitating and traumatic. When that is the case, the pain and injury must be addressed before moving forward. I was involved with two groups, one of Native American activists and the other of environmental activists, who were in negotiation related to important land use issues. The main woman representing the Native American group—I'll call her Sally—made a number of demands of the environmentalist group, including that the tribe have representatives on decision-making bodies going forward. The effort to bridge the differences between the two groups had been going on for several months.

After some back and forth, all the parties seemed to agree on the terms. I was elated, as I thought the issue was very important and had relationships with both groups.

When I reported the breakthough of the environmental group to Sally, I was very pleased. Virtually all the conditions the tribe had been asking for were agreed to, and there was a substantial amount of money and land at issue.

Then something happened that surprised me. Sally stated she would not allow the agreement to go forth. She said she did not trust the environmentalists involved. I was confused and shocked. Sally had been active thoughout the effort, and what was agreed to largely aligned with what she had been pushing for. After a number of conversations following Sally's rejection of the agreement, she shared something critical for me to understand. She noted that throughout the entire process, no apology had been offered for what white people had done to the tribe. For Sally, it simply was not possible to move forward until there was a recognition of the hurt and an apology. We could not move to a solution without acknowledging the injury.

It was not enough to have an agreement—the need to be seen and recognized, including her feelings and dignity, was crucial. Sometimes the beginning of healing is recognizing someone else's suffering.

I am sometimes asked what is most important to focus on: is it the journey or the destination? I have learned that, at least for me, it is the company I keep. I have been blessed with awesome company and profound love. Still, I carry my suffering and the suffering of people I love.

There is also a difference between emotions and feelings. Neither is solid, and they are often a composite. Feelings are sometimes described as emotions meeting thought. Another way to say it is that feelings take their form in part according to the story we wrap emotions in. Feelings with the meaning that comes from a story give a shape to what we call emotions. I am not suggesting that we move away from a feeling because it is painful, but we should also pay attention to the story about the feeling.

Spirituality as I practice it is about making space, not pushing away. A child's feelings and emotions are more likely to move because they are not held as tightly as an adult would in a story of the mind. We all know what it's like to have more than one feeling or emotion at the same time. The word *ambivalent* understates how normal this process is. I suggest that we not push our feelings away but give them space. Let them flow.

The converse is also true. We should not insist on holding onto our feelings and emotions. One of the ways to describe trauma is as frozen emotions. This suggests, I believe correctly, that in a healthy state our emotions and feelings flow.

We can help each other in this process by reminding each other of the fullness of life. While we might be dealing with difficulties, life is that and more. Why would we hold onto something that gives us pain? Because it may also be giving us meaning. And we are meaning-making beings. Not having meaning or not belonging with a group that gives us meaning might cause great pain.

As I shared at the beginning of this book, my parents' lives, and in many ways my early life as well, were full of joy, love, *and* very hard circumstances. There were times I only held onto the difficulty. I hope I can now respect that as just one of many aspects of my life at any given time. As I write these words, I worry about the world *and* am deeply in love with my children, including my baby girl.

Reflect

- How might seeing yourself as part of the world, changing as it changes, shape your day-to-day actions? Your willingness to attempt to bridge or not?

- Do you see yourself as separate from others or connected?

- What are the key values that guide your life? What are the key values you see guiding the organizations and institutions you are part of?

- How might the ideas in this book encourage you to embrace the fullness of life?

Conclusion

Becoming a Bridger

As I come to the final chapter of this book, I realize it is about *being* a bridger as much as it is about bridging itself.

That is because I am a bridger, or at least that is my orientation. That was not always true, and it's not always strictly true now. Sometimes I am an advocate. Sometimes I am a father. Sometimes I am just waiting to see what part of me will surface. I try not to be afraid of my amygdala, and I hope this book uncovers ideas and concepts that help you not be afraid of yours. Fear is natural, but bridging is a choice.

I have spent much time on the *promise and potential* of bridging and on being or becoming a bridger. I hope I have made a case for the importance of bridging and belonging and raised some deeper considerations as one considers how to practice bridging. In the Resources I have also shared information on some groups who are doing bridging work that I recommend.

I also recognize that you are probably reading this book because you are interested in getting started. If you want to bridge, what should you do? Before I close with some ideas on how to approach that question, I will share that I do have a degree of skepticism of technique. Techniques can too often become ends in themselves if they are unmoored to values or a deep practice. Techniques without an overarching vision rooted in values can become meaningless and even dehumanizing.

So while I caution against approaching bridging as a set of boxes to check, I believe the power of bridging itself is that it moves us away from technique and into a deeper way of considering relationships and the world. Bridging will not only help us to understand ourselves and each other better, but will also help us to be more engaged and open with ourselves and the world. Bridging helps us create the conditions to make better decisions about the world we want to create. Bridging does not deny our suffering or the suffering of others, but it builds a space where we can suffer and dream together.

Bridging is not about being civil but about being respectful both of the other and of ourselves. We don't have to deny our feelings or any conflict between us and others. But we do not allow this to dampen our interest in and curiosity about the other.

I suggested earlier in the book that bridging may require an act of faith. We may take precautions when engaging the other and try to set up some agreements. When I am approached about long bridges, I will make it clear that violence has to be off limits. This requirement can be extended beyond just physical violence. Even small agreements can began to build guardrails and trust. But it is not possible to establish a guarantee of complete safety and trust beforehand. This lack of complete trust and safety may cause us to hold back from bridging. And yet, without allowing ourselves some exposure, without tolerating some vulnerability, the possibility of bridging will be very limited. This is where an act of faith comes in, along with the possibility of grace. Am I willing to extend a trusting hand to the other in hopes that they will do the same?

I am not suggesting that one be either blind or foolish. I am saying one must access one's capacity to be vulnerable.

Bridging is also not everything or nothing. We might start with short bridges or with bridges that are relatively easy. But we don't stay there.

As we become more comfortable and the bridging muscle gets stronger, we can take on more difficult situations. At some point we might shift from simply engaging in bridging to become a bridger. But just as we must extend grace to others, we must also extend grace to ourselves. We are human. We will make mistakes.

Despite this book not being one of technique, I want to close with a few practices one might engage in to help support bridging and belonging. This is not meant to be an exhaustive inventory. What's on your list?

1. Move Toward Being.

Let's start with a concept my friend Ben McBride has shared with me: Perhaps our starting place doesn't have to be asking, "What do we want to do?" but asking instead, "Whom do we want to be?" Bridging begins there.

When bridging, try to move from interests to values to being. This is aligned with moving from transactional to transformational to spiritual.

We express our values naturally when we feel heard or safe enough. When we talk with someone, we don't usually say, "Okay, now let's talk about our values." When you talk from a place of bridging, and set an intention to bridge, and have curiosity and openness, the other person may naturally want to tell you about their life, about their hard times, about the time when they didn't get the job they wanted, when their dog died, or when their mother fell ill. In other words, when we are open to listening to who the person is, rather than what their position is on something, they will tell you about their life and their suffering.

But when we start off by first identifying someone as an opponent or as someone who needs to be won over on any number of issues, we may miss the chance to get to *being*. In many ways, to flatten a person to a single quality is to deny their their fullness and their complexity—in other words, their beingness. In this path we probably won't get to shared values, missing a number of potential ways and places for us to connect. With this approach, we are more likely to focus on our place of disconnect. We focus on whether the policy you want and the one I want, or the party you'll vote for or the one I'll vote for, are different.

When we fail to allow for even the possibility to create a bridge, we ignore the fact that we're talking with people who also have concerns and suffering just like we do. We miss the possibility of realizing that our underlying values may be similar. We can approach the *other* with real curiosity at the *being* level. Who are they? What is important to them in their lives? How have they suffered? What are their hopes and fears? One should as much as possible listen with the heart and not the analytical mind.

The more vital consideration is that when we take the time to understand people, many of the disagreements that felt fundamental may go away or at least take on a different feeling or significance.

When we bridge, we leave open the possibility to create a container to hold disagreements and hold space for one another.

2. Be Open to a More Complex Story.

When we meet virtually anyone, we almost immediately create a story in our head. We assume what the person is like. We assume many things that we could not possibly know upon the first meeting. This story making happens at an unconscious level faster than the speed of consciousness—much faster. Even as this story develops, we may or may not be aware of it.

We read cues about the other person's environment and make assumptions. We also create a story about them based on things we have picked up from our own social environment. This is the heart of stereotype.

This rapid, unconscious process creates both positive and negative stories. It has been suggested we could not survive without these unconscious processes. We are not in complete control of our consciousness, nor are we completely controlled by it. Being aware of the stories we're telling about other people creates a foundation for bridging.

One of the fundamental necessities in bridging is to *slow down and attend.* To attend to the emerging story in our head as well as to how the body is feeling. To attend to our intentions.

To attend requires presence. Many of the stories take us away from what is happening in the moment. Paying attention to the stories we're telling heightens our attention but can be challenging, especially if we have don't practice.

Knowing about how the unconsious works may help us prepare. We can become aware that we don't normally come in contact with this other and that we therefore carry stories about them that may or may not be true. We need to be open both to them and to our own feelings and values.

Many groups working to reduce polarization and division suggest first setting an intention to bridge, starting within oneself. "How do I feel when I think of the other?" Feel how you feel. While I support this practice, I also would add to that. There are times when starting with yourself will not be available to you. I would caution against the intention to first fix or even know oneself and *then* engage with the world. We have to find ways to do both at the same time.

3. Make Others Feel Seen.

Belonging means being fully seen. One of the most effective ways to bridge is letting the other know that they have been seen. So often the lizard brain is screaming for fear of not being seen.

You may ask, as many do, "But what about *my* needs? Why should it be placed on me to bridge? My lizard brain is also screaming." Yes, you should care for your safety, but bridging is not about disappearing or retreating.

We may start with the Zulu phrase *Sawubona*, which translates as "I see you." This means the divine in me sees the divine in you.

You may want to set up agreements at the beginning. "I really want to know more about you and share more about myself. Why don't one of us start, and the other will listen and ask questions, and then we will switch?" "Let's not talk about the election or politics until later."

The signal is: "I am interested in you. I hope you are interested in me as well." Look for common human ground. To be a bridger means to at least create the chance to find or make common ground. Rather than an outcome where winners make the rules and the losers go home (if such a separate place exists), in a world of bridging we strive toward the belief that there are no losers.

Bridging doesn't mean that you must agree with or even like someone. But it does mean you recognize the other person's humanity. Bridging helps us move from dichotomies or binaries to multiplicities and multitudes. To explore and identify these multiplicities takes curiosity and openness. Bridging helps us see conflict in a different way. When people see one another's humanity, they are likely to attend to that and not just to wondering who will win. Is there a way we might both win?

Bridging is calling for a future that brings us closer together without requiring us to be the same. Instead of denying or ignoring the fact that people have different pasts or are situated differently in the present, bridging means we create additional space where we recognize our differences and our commonality without denying either. As I noted earlier, it is only because of our sameness *and* difference that dialogue is possible. It is this dynamic of sameness and difference that makes bridging desirable.

4. Practice.

Work out the muscle of bridging. The more you do it, the stronger it gets, as long as we remain open to experimenting and to the possibilities that present themselves.

Bridging does not have to be a perfectly balanced exchange each time. Experienced bridgers will likely confirm that it often isn't. Yet the power of practicing bridging benefits the whole community.

While there is a growing bridging movement, some of whose stories I've included in this book, this work has trouble gaining currency in our news cycles and discourse, both public and private, which tend to focus on problems, disasters, and breaking stories rather than on positive stories and connection. We must find a way to change that. I hope this book helps in that effort.

5. Understand Group and Power Dynamics.

There is bridging between individuals and between groups, and the impact and risk are often quite different. Being attuned to those differences and the impact that they have may help. Consider the role of power in the respective groups open to bridging. What might be appropriate in one context may not be in another. In groups, we may want to start with shorter bridges. In general, I encourage us to be hard on systems and soft on people.

Groups looking to bridge may want to set up agreements and guardrails. Powerful bridging can happen when people come together under the right conditions and with a common purpose.

Think of a situation where the two groups depend on each other to succeed instead of staying in a winner-takes-all competition.

6. Consider Different Types of Bridging.

There are bridges between loved ones and family. These bridges can feel especially vulnerable. Interfamily bridging can take place over longer periods of time than bridging between other types of individuals or groups. And, as discussed earlier, there is bridging that is transactional, there is bridging that is transformational, and there is bridging that is an expression of our most profound spiritual aspirations.

7. Remove or Reduce Threats That Lead to Breaking.

When building a long bridge, try to remove or reduce any deep ontological threats or what are perceived as threats to someone else's very being. One of the biggest barriers to bridging is the implicit assertion that not only is the other group wrong but they are fundamentally bad. Look for less threatening common ground before addressing more difficult issues.

8. Remember to Breathe and Be Kind to the Earth and to All Beings, Including Yourself.

Living in a world where we are often not seen or where breaking has become a default way of being can take a mental, physical, and spiritual toll. We may respond defensively by also breaking with others or just shutting down. But even strategies to try to stay safe take a toll. Being kind to the world includes being kind to ourselves.

I am suggesting a couple of things here. The first is to remember to breathe. I mean a deep, soulful breath that puts us back in touch with our bodies. Such a type of breath can do more than just bring us oxygen: it can allow us to be present and relax and even heal or move toward it.

Some of you may not be ready to bridge or even to become bridgers. So here is the second suggestion. For those of you who are not ready to bridge, I would ask you to at least consider not breaking.

The good news is that once you have decided to begin the process to deliberately become a bridger, you are already on your way. If you decide to engage with the power of bridging, welcome to the journey. It is a place of possibility and life. You are not alone. You will be welcomed by other bridgers, some human and some not. Join us in not just meeting the other but meeting the other in me. Join us in creating a world where all belong and none are othered. I look forward to meeting us there.

Acknowledgments from
john a. powell

There are many people who have helped me write this book and have had a substantial impact on how I think about bridging and being a bridger. I would like to thank them all, even the ones I do not name in this space.

I would like to start by acknowledging my late parents and my family. My mother, Florcie Mae Rimpson Powell, and my father, Marshall Powell Jr., taught me invaluable lessons about bridging and so much more. And my siblings, including my late brothers Gary and Ray Powell, as well as Cledos Powell, Eunice Graves, Barbara Jarrells, Peggy Wortmann, Freida Webster, and Robin Harris; and my children, Saneta DeVuono-powell, Fon DeVuono-powell, and Simone Grace powell—all have been close to the learnings of bridging and breaking in the circle of love and disappointment that all families entail.

This book is more than just a conceptual meditation on bridging—it reflects real-life work in bridging. In this regard I would like to thank the staff of the Othering & Belonging Institute (OBI). The book reflects not only my own personal experience but what we learned at OBI by together trying bridging in the world and working to sharpen the meanings and practices of bridging. Special acknowledgment goes out to Rachelle Galloway-Popotas, Stephen Menendian, Gerald Lenoir, Olivia Araiza, Eloy Toppin, Joshua Clark, and Cecilie Surasky.

Rachelle Galloway-Popotas came to the book at a later stage and made insightful additions that brought the book to life and completion. Her efforts went beyond that of editing. What was partially at work with Rachelle was a deep understanding of the spiritual nature of bridging and being able to hear and help translate my voice.

Stephen Menendian has helped over the years to deepen my approach to bridging and othering and belonging, both conceptually and in practice.

Gerald Lenoir and Olivia Araiza were key to helping the institute's bridging work gain traction. For years they have worked with people in civic engagement and grassroots movements who were skeptical of bridging, but they kept up the effort until they found a way to make it work. In the process, they gave bridging legs in the communities we were engaged with and beyond.

I want to acknowledge Eloy Toppin and Joshua Clark for helping with research and with furthering our understanding of bridging and power. Eloy shone a light on how the dynamics of bridging change when focusing on groups and institutions instead of individuals. Josh has provided valuable insight on fragmentation and polarization, and how they differ.

I would like to thank Cecilie Surasky, who has expanded OBI's bridging and belonging work through public education efforts and her commitment to building long bridges between Palestinians and Jews.

Thank you to Tatum Hurley and Julia McKeown at OBI for their research and assistance on the resources and reflection questions.

I want to thank Karen Bouris, who helped birth the idea of doing a book on bridging with Tami Simon at Sounds True and who worked on earlier drafts with a focus on the possible audience for this book.

Thank you to Courtney Wooten, who helped with stories and examples that would best reflect bridging.

I would also like to thank Alana and Ned Conner, who gave useful feedback, inspiration, and a close read.

I would also like to acknowledge Valarie Kaur, whose work on radical love and the rejection of the very idea of the *other* helped influence my own work in this area.

I would also like to thank and acknowledge Heather McGee, whose work on bridging and connecting to those who are different has been a bright light in the growing bridging world.

I want to thank Rachel Godsil, who has been an important teacher and friend. I have learned a great deal about mind science from Rachel and her work at the Perception Institute, a consortium of advocates who were and continue to be early adopters in the bridging field, backed by empirical research.

I have also learned a lot from friend and neuroscientist Tanya Singer's work in bringing mind science research into bridging, especially her efforts to address the difference between empathetic and compassionate listening.

I would also like to thank Deepak Bhargava as being one of the first people to point out the problems associated with short bridges.

Thank you to DeAngelo Bester for being an activist on the ground who moved his work to addressing long bridges.

I want to acknowledge Arthur Brooks, who helped make bridging less of a chore and more of an intimate exchange with a friend.

I would also like to thank Michael McBride and Ben McBride, both of whom have taken up the challenge of bridging in a spiritual and political space. Their work and conversations were helpful not only in clarifying issues for this book but also in advancing the bridging community.

I would also like to acknowledge and thank Loretta Ross, who taught me valuable lessons about healing and bridging.

I would like to acknowledge Angela Glover-Blackwell and Michael McAfee for helping to raise the issue of how bridging works in a racially charged environment.

I would like to thank Joan Blades of Living Room Conversations for providing valuable insight on bridging.

I would also like to acknowledge friends and bridging partners at the Greater Good Science Center at University of California, Berkeley.

I would like to thank More in Common, whose cofounders Tim Dixon, Gemma Mortensen, and Mathieu Lefevre have been key in helping me understand many of the nuances of bridging in several different countries.

I would also like to thank and acknowledge the New Pluralists, who have been partners and supporters for bridging on this journey.

I want to also thank Sarah Stephens for inviting me into her bridging work through CareLab.

I want to acknowledge the work of journalist and podcast host Krista Tippett; a conversation I had with Krista on her show *On Being* helped me better articulate some of my work on bridging.

There are numerous others who helped in the development of the ideas in the book. I would like to acknowledge and thank all of you as well as those of you who have practiced bridging in your daily life.

Acknowledgments from
Rachelle Galloway-Popotas

Thank you to all my colleagues at the Othering & Belonging Institute who have taught me so much through our work bending the arc toward belonging. I am especially grateful to those who have created spaces of love and learning in our work together and who never saw those as separate endeavors: Puanani Forbes, Cecilie Surasky, Olivia Araiza, Marc Abizeid, Basima Sisemore, Sara Grossman, Stephen Menendian, Michael Omi, Gerald Lenoir, Josh Clark, Nadia Barhoum, Evan Bissell, Elsadig Elsheikh, Eli Moore, Rasheed Shabazz, and Rachel Parsons. Thank you to Connie Cagampang Heller, who provided compassionate mentoring during a critical juncture of my work at OBI. I want to acknowledge Phenocia Bauerle at University of California, Berkeley, who extended belonging and bridging to me in the Native American community. I want to acknowledge the work of Naomi Klein, especially her book *No Logo*, which altered my professional course and gave me a political home. I am grateful to Sarah Stanton at Sounds True for being such a gracious, generous, and positive editor. Thank you to Jade Lascelles at Sounds True for her skillfull and sharp editorial expertise in helping polish the book to completion. Enormous gratitude goes to Tatum Hurley for her deep research and review assistance. Thank you to Frances England for a lifetime of friendship and for being the most natural bridge builder I know. Thank you to my parents for keeping the commitment of love constant despite our many differences.

Thank you to Vassili, Juno, and Zenon, whose love has always made everything else possible. Finally, I want to acknowledge john a. powell for his visionary and radically egalitarian leadership and the depth of his intellectual and spiritual contributions. I also want to thank him for the invitation he has extended not only to me but to everyone to be part of this life-affirming and world-making journey that is bridging.

Resources

Bridging Organizations

American Talks

mycountrytalks.org/events/america-talks

An effort matching thousands of Americans who hold political differences into small group conversations with the goal of helping shift perspectives from "us versus them" to "you and me." USA.

BridgeUSA

bridgeusa.org

A youth-led 501(c)(3) nonprofit organization that creates spaces on high school and college campuses for open discussion among students about political issues. USA.

Care Lab

carelab.org

An organization facilitating community conversations to address the crisis of polarization in the United States. USA.

CoGenerate

cogenerate.org

A bridging organization bringing people across all ages to work together intentionally. USA.

Conflict Transformation Lab: The Power of Dialogue

ctl.georgetown.edu/programs/pod

An immersive dialogue experience that brings together university students to bridge the gap between rural and urban communities. USA.

Constructive Dialogue Institute

constructivedialogue.org

A research institute that develops educational tools and frameworks for bridging political divisions. USA.

Dinner & Dialogue

dinnersanddialogue.com

A project that uses food to bring people together, foster mutual understanding, and bridge divisions in society. USA.

Disagree Better

nga.org/disagree-better

An initiative by the National Governors Association providing governors with resources to facilitate conversations that counter polarization and hyperpartisanship. USA.

GORM Media

gormmedia.com

Social enterprise organization using digital media and intercultural training to bring groups together across differences and advance belonging for marginalized communities. Ireland.

Greater Good Science Center

greatergood.berkeley.edu

Explores the science of happiness and a meaningful life through research and outreach programs. Based at University of California, Berkeley. USA.

Humanize

humanize.com

A digital platform that fosters self-growth, connection, and mental health for people and companies. Luxembourg.

Living Room Conversations

livingroomconversations.org

An organization facilitating connection and understanding across divides through a variety of conversation resources and services. USA.

Millions of Conversations

millionsofconversations.com

A media-driven campaign designed to change existing narratives that marginalize and politicize "the other." Starting with the predominating narrative about Muslim Americans, their focus is on eliminating stigma in all its forms. USA.

More in Common

moreincommon.com

A research initiative that aims to address the underlying factors that create polarization in society and work toward a more collective and resilient world. USA, UK, Poland, Germany, and France.

National Institute for Civil Discourse

nicd.arizona.edu

A nonpartisan organization working to promote healthy and civil political debate. Based at the University of Arizona. USA.

New Pluralists

newpluralists.org

A funder collaborative focused on renewing the promise of pluralism in America in order to realize our promise of becoming a politically vibrant, multiracial, multifaith democracy. USA.

+972 Magazine

972mag.com

+972 is an independent, online, nonprofit magazine run by a group of Palestinian and Israeli journalists. Founded in 2010, their mission is to provide in-depth reporting, analysis, and opinions from the ground in Israel-Palestine. The name of the site is derived from the telephone country code that can be used to dial throughout Israel-Palestine.

The On Being Project

onbeing.org

Founded by Krista Tippett, the On Being Project is an ongoing dialogue in multiple media that explores questions of what it means to be human and how we can live in community with one another. USA.

Sacred Design Lab

sacred.design

A research and development lab that aims to understand and design for twenty-first-century spiritual well-being by translating ancient wisdom and practices to help their partners develop products, programs, and experiences that ground people's social and spiritual lives.

Search for Common Ground

sfcg.org

The largest dedicated peace-building organization in the world. Aims to transform the way the world deals with conflict, away from adversarial approaches and toward cooperative solutions, and their vision is a world where cooperation is the norm—where differences stimulate social progress, rather than precipitate violence.

Spaceship Media

spaceshipmedia.org

Dialogue journalism designed to bridge divides, with projects on gun safety, racial educational gaps, immigration, SROs, and more. USA.

Weave: The Social Fabric Project

weavers.org

Founded by author and journalist David Brooks, Weave aims to connect, lift, and inspire communities to address the crisis of isolation in the United States. USA.

Writings on Bridging

Bridging Differences Playbook by the Greater Good Science Center, greatergood.berkeley.edu/images/uploads/Bridging _Differences_Playbook-Final.pdf

I Never Thought of It That Way: How to Have Fearlessly Curious Conversations in Dangerously Divided Times by Mónica Guzmán

On Bridging: Evidence and Guidance from Real World Cases by john a. powell and Rachel Heydemann, belonging.berkeley .edu/on-bridging

Seek: How Curiosity Can Transform Your Life and Change the World by Scott Shigeoka

We Need to Build: Field Notes for Diverse Democracy by Eboo Patel

Digital and Video Resources on Bridging

Bridging and Breaking Curriculum by Ashley Gallegos, Gerald Lenoir, Miriam Magaña Lopez, and Tanya Díaz, OBI University, belonging.berkeley.edu/bridging-breaking -curriculum

"Bridging: Towards a Society Built on Belonging," Othering & Belonging Institute, youtube.com/watch?v=MZjSsuz1yfA

A Call to Connection: Rediscovering the Transformative Power of Relationships, Einhorn Collaborative, Greater Good Science Center, and Sacred Design Lab, einhorncollaborative.org/call -to-connection

"Calling In: A Conversation with Loretta J. Ross," SNF Agora Institute at Johns Hopkins University, youtube.com/watch?v= NwAPvI9Kn_M

"Garden Conversation: The Risk and Possibility of Bridging," with john a. powell and Judith Butler, Othering & Belonging Institute, youtube.com/watch?v=NGG1du0FK0w

"How Cross-Cultural Understanding Can Help Us to See Each Other," TEDx Talk by Simone Buijzen, youtube.com/watch?v=XvjaIrYlkIg&t=2s

"Lesson 4: How to Bridge," OBI University, obiu.org/course/how-to-bridge

"Worlds Apart," Publicis London for Heineken, youtube.com/watch?v=IbIjGxc1vjo

Selected Bibliography

Chapter 1: Bridging to the Future

Geertz, Clifford. *Local Knowledge: Further Essays in Interpretive Anthropology*. New York: Basic Books, 2008.

Kimmerer, Robin Wall. *Braiding Sweetgrass: Indigenous Wisdom, Scientific Knowledge, and the Teaching of Plants*. Minneapolis: Milkweed Editions, 2013.

Krawec, Patty. *Becoming Kin: An Indigenous Call to Unforgetting the Past and Reimagining Our Future*. Minneapolis: Broadleaf Books, 2022.

powell, john a. *Racing to Justice: Transforming Our Conceptions of Self and Other to Build an Inclusive Society*. Bloomington: Indiana University Press, 2012.

Public Religion Research Institute. *Threats to American Democracy Ahead of an Unprecedented Presidential Election*. October 25, 2023. prri.org/research/threats-to-american-democracy-ahead -of-an-unprecedented-presidential-election/.

Chapter 2: The Problem Is Othering

Allen, Theodore W. *The Invention of the White Race: The Origin of Racial Oppression*. New York: Verso Books, 2022.

Anderson, Abigail, Sophia Chilczuk, Kaylie Nelson, Roxanne Ruther, and Cara Wall-Scheffler. "The Myth of Man the Hunter: Women's Contribution to the Hunt Across Ethnographic Contexts." *PLOS One* 18, no. 6 (2023). doi.org/10.1371/journal.pone.0287101.

Baldwin, James. *Selected Articles from 'The Price of the Ticket: Collected Nonfiction, 1948–1985.'* New York: St. Martin's/Marek, 1985.

de Beauvoir, Simone. *The Second Sex.* Paris: Éditions Gallimard, 1949. Translated by Constance Borde and Sheila Malovany-Chevallier. New York: Vintage Books, 2011.

Du Bois, W. E. B. *The Souls of Black Folk.* Chicago: A. C. McClurg, 1903.

Graeber, David, and David Wengrow. *The Dawn of Everything: A New History of Humanity.* New York: Farrar, Straus and Giroux, 2021.

Ignatiev, Noel. *How the Irish Became White.* New York: Routledge, 1995.

Kerner, Otto, John V. Lindsay, Fred R. Harris, Edward W. Brooke, James C. Corman, William M. McCulloch, I. W. Abel, et al. *Report of the National Advisory Commission on Civil Disorders.* New York: Bantam Books, 1968. belonging.berkeley.edu/sites/default/files/kerner_commission_full_report.pdf?file=1&force=1.

Lamont, Michèle. *Seeing Others: How Recognition Works—and How It Can Heal a Divided World.* New York: One Signal Publishers / Atria, 2023.

López, Ian Haney. *White by Law: The Legal Construction of Race.* New York: New York University Press, 2006.

Martinot, Steve. *Rules of Racialization: Class, Identity, Governance.* Philadelphia: Temple University Press, 2003.

Marx, Anthony W. *Making Race and Nation: A Comparison of South Africa, the United States, and Brazil.* Cambridge, UK: Cambridge University Press, 1998.

Massey, Douglas. *Categorically Unequal: The American Stratification System.* New York: Russell Sage Foundation, 2007.

McMahon, Darrin M. *Equality: The History of an Elusive Idea.* New York: Basic Books, 2023.

Myrdal, Gunnar. *An American Dilemma: The Negro Problem and Modern Democracy.* New York: Harper & Row, 1944.

Ocobock, Cara, and Sarah Lacy. "Woman the Hunter." *Scientific American* 329, no. 4 (2023): 22.

Omi, Michael, and Howard Winant. *Racial Formation in the United States.* New York: Routledge, 1994.

Said, Edward. *Orientalism.* New York: Vintage Books, 1979.

Sapolsky, Robert. *Behave: The Biology of Humans at Our Best and Worst.* New York: Penguin Books, 2018.

Chapter 3: Is Othering Natural?

Banaji, Mahzarin R., and Anthony G. Greenwald. *Blindspot: Hidden Biases of Good People.* New York: Delacorte Press, 2013.

Brown, Brené. *Atlas of the Heart: Mapping Meaningful Connection and the Language of Human Experience.* New York: Random House, 2021.

———. *Daring Greatly: How the Courage to Be Vulnerable Transforms the Way We Live, Love, Parent, and Lead.* New York: Avery, 2012.

Butler, Judith. *The Force of Nonviolence: An Ethico-Political Bind.* New York: Verso Books, 2020.

Cohen, Geoffrey L. *Belonging: The Science of Creating Connection and Bridging Divides.* New York: W. W. Norton, 2022.

Gadamer, Hans-Georg. "Language and Understanding." *Theory, Culture, & Society* 23, no. 1 (2006): 13–27. doi.org/10.1177 /0263276406063226.

Maslow, Abraham H. "A Theory of Human Motivation." *Psychological Review* 50, no. 4 (1943): 370–96. doi.org/10 .1037/h0054346.

Minow, Martha. *Making All the Difference: Inclusion, Exclusion, and American Law.* Ithaca, NY: Cornell University Press, 1990.

Mitchell, Maurice. "Building Resilient Organizations." *The Forge*, November 29, 2022. forgeorganizing.org/article/building -resilient-organizations.

powell, john a., and Ece Temelkuran. "Reimagining What's Possible: From Authoritarianism and Othering to Democracy and Belonging." Video recording. Othering & Belonging Conference, October 26, 2023, Berlin, Germany. youtube .com/watch?v=tQYSY0oUoSE&t=9260s.

Sapolsky, Robert. *Behave: The Biology of Humans at Our Best and Worst.* New York: Penguin Books, 2018.

Solomon, Andrew. *Far from the Tree: Parents, Children, and the Search for Identity.* New York: Scribner, 2012.

Tajfel, Henri. "Experiments in Intergroup Discrimination." *Scientific American* 223, no. 5 (1970): 96–103. jstor.org/stable /24927662.

Unger, Roberto M. *False Necessity: Anti-Necessitarian Social Theory in the Service of Radical Democracy.* New York: Verso Books, 2004.

Williams, Robert A., Jr. *Savage Anxieties: The Invention of Western Civilization.* New York: St. Martin's Press, 2012.

Chapter 4: Breaking and Othering

Armstrong, Karen. *Sacred Nature: Restoring Our Ancient Bond with the Natural World.* New York: Alfred A. Knopf, 2022.

Cuddy, Amy J. C., Susan T. Fiske, Virginia S. Y. Kwan, Peter Glick, Stéphanie Demoulin, Jacques-Philippe Leyens,

Michael Harris Bond, et al. "Stereotype Content Model Across Cultures: Towards Universal Similarities and Some Differences." *British Journal of Social Psychology* 48 (2009): 1–33. doi.org/10.1348/014466608X314935.

Eberhardt, Jennifer. *Bias: Uncovering the Hidden Prejudice That Shapes What We See, Think, and Do.* New York: Viking, 2019.

Eberhardt, Jennifer, Phillip Atiba Goff, Valerie J. Purdie, and Paul G. Davies. "Seeing Black: Race, Crime, and Visual Processing." *Journal of Personality and Social Psychology* 87, no. 6 (2004): 876–93.

Fiske, Susan T., Amy J. C. Cuddy, Peter Glick, and Jun Xu. "A Model of (Often Mixed) Stereotype Content: Competence and Warmth Respectively Follow from Perceived Status and Competition." *Journal of Personality and Social Psychology* 82, no. 6 (2002): 878–902.

Graeber, David, and David Wengrow. *The Dawn of Everything: A New History of Humanity.* New York: Farrar, Straus and Giroux, 2021.

McMahon, Darrin M. *Equality: The History of an Elusive Idea.* New York: Basic Books, 2023.

Chapter 5: Hard and Soft Breaking

Chen, M. Keith, and Ryne Rohla. "The Effect of Partisanship and Political Advertising on Close Family Ties." *Science* 360, no. 6392 (2018): 1020–24. science.org/doi/epdf/10.1126/science.aaq1433.

Kaur, Valarie. *See No Stranger: A Memoir and Manifesto of Revolutionary Love.* New York: Penguin Random House, 2020.

Putnam, Robert. *Bowling Alone: The Collapse and Revival of American Community.* New York: Simon & Schuster, 2000.

Sen, Amartya. *Development as Freedom*. New York: Anchor Books, 1999.

Chapter 6: On Belonging

Graeber, David, and David Wengrow. *The Dawn of Everything: A New History of Humanity*. New York: Farrar, Straus and Giroux, 2021.

Maalouf, Amin. *In the Name of Identity: Violence and the Need to Belong*. Translated by Barbara Bray. New York: Arcade Publishing, 1998.

powell, john a. "Transformative Action: A Strategy for Ending Racial Hierarchy and Achieving True Democracy." In *Beyond Racism: Race and Inequality in Brazil, South Africa, and the United States*. Edited by Charles Hamilton, Lynn Huntley, Neville Alexander, Antonio Sérgio Alfredo Guimarães, and Wilmot James. Boulder, CO: Lynne Rienner Publishers, 2001.

powell, john a., and Stephen Menendian. *Belonging without Othering: How We Save Ourselves and the World*. Stanford, CA: Stanford University Press, 2024.

Rawls, John. *A Theory of Justice*. Cambridge, MA: Belknap Press, 1971.

Ripley, Amanda. *High Conflict: Why We Get Trapped and How We Get Out*. New York: Simon & Schuster, 2021.

Unger, Roberto. *Passion: An Essay on Personality*. New York: Free Press, 1984.

Chapter 7: Understanding Bridging

Baldwin, James. "Here Be Dragons." *Playboy*, January 1985.

Baldwin, James, and Margaret Mead. *A Rap on Race*. New York: Dell Publishing, 1972.

Crenshaw, Kimberlé. "Demarginalizing the Intersection of Race and Sex: A Black Feminist Critique of Antidiscrimination Doctrine, Feminist Theory, and Antiracist Politics." *University of Chicago Legal Forum* 1989, no. 1 (1989). chicagounbound .uchicago.edu/uclf/vol1989/iss1/8.

Diamond, Jared. *Collapse: How Societies Choose to Fail or Succeed.* New York: Viking, 2005.

Leigh Fermor, Patrick. *Abducting a General: The Kreipe Operation in Crete.* New York: New York Review Books, 2014.

Machado de Oliveira, Vanessa. *Hospicing Modernity: Facing Humanity's Wrongs and the Implications for Social Activism.* Berkeley, CA: North Atlantic Books, 2021.

Massey, Douglas. *Categorically Unequal: The American Stratification System.* New York: Russell Sage Foundation, 2007.

Mitchell, Maurice. "Building Resilient Organizations. *The Forge,* November 29, 2022. orgeorganizing.org/article/building -resilient-organizations.

Putnam, Robert. *Bowling Alone: The Collapse and Revival of American Community.* New York: Simon & Schuster, 2000.

Rusk, David. "The 'Segregation Tax': The Cost of Racial Segregation to Black Homeowners." Brookings Institution, Center on Urban & Metropolitan Policy, October 2001. brookings.edu/wp-content/uploads/2016/06/rusk.pdf.

Sapolsky, Robert. *Behave: The Biology of Humans at Our Best and Worst.* New York: Penguin Books, 2018.

Steele, Claude, and Joshua Aronson. "Stereotype Threat and the Intellectual Test Performance of African Americans." *Journal of Personality and Social Psychology* 69, no. 5 (1995): 797–811.

Weber, Max. *On Charisma and Institution Building: Selected Writings.* Edited by S. N. Eisenstadt. Chicago: University of Chicago Press, 1968.

Young, Iris Marion. *Inclusion and Democracy.* Oxford, UK: Oxford University Press, 2000.

Chapter 8: Short and Long Bridges

"Loretta Ross: Calling-In the Call-Out Culture." *Pulling the Thread with Elise Loehnen.* Podcast episode, September 23, 2021. eliseloehnen.com/episodes/loretta-ross.

Page, Scott E. *The Diversity Bonus: How Great Teams Pay Off in the Knowledge Economy.* Princeton, NJ: Princeton University Press, 2017.

Roediger, David. *The Wages of Whiteness: Race and the Making of the American Working Class.* New York: Verso Books, 2022.

"Toxic Polarization: The Latest Numbers." Listen First Project, 2022. listenfirstproject.org/toxic-polarization-data.

Chapter 9: Bridging and Spirituality

Kaur, Valarie. *See No Stranger: A Memoir and Manifesto of Revolutionary Love.* New York: Penguin Random House, 2020.

Kropotkin, Peter. *Mutual Aid: A Factor of Evolution.* New York: McClure Phillips, 1902.

Macy, Joanna. *World as Lover, World as Self: Courage for Global Justice and Ecological Renewal.* Berkeley, CA: Parallax Press, 2007.

Nhat Hahn, Thich. *Interbeing: Fourteen Guidelines for Engaged Buddhism.* Berkeley, CA: Parallax Press, 1998.

Schopenhauer, Arthur. *Parerga and Paralipomena.* Vol. 2, *Short Philosophical Essays.* 1851. Reprint, Cambridge, UK: Cambridge University Press, 2015.

Index

About the Author

j ohn a. powell (who spells his name in lowercase in the belief that we should be part of the universe, not over it) is a renowned scholar of civil rights, civil liberties, structural racialization, housing, poverty, and democracy. He is the director of the Othering & Belonging Institute at the University of California, Berkeley, where he holds the Robert D. Haas Chancellor's Chair in Equity and Inclusion. john is also a professor of law, African American studies, and ethnic studies at UC Berkeley. He has previously held posts as executive director of the Kirwan Institute for the Study of Race and Ethnicity at Ohio State University, where he was also the Gregory H. Williams Chair in Civil Rights and Civil Liberties at the Moritz College of Law; founder and director of the Institute on Race and Poverty at the University of Minnesota Law School; cofounder of the Perception Institute; the director of legal services in Miami, Florida; and the national legal director of the American Civil Liberties Union. john has lived and worked in Africa, India, and Brazil as well as the United States and has taught at numerous law schools, including Harvard University and Columbia University. He serves on the boards of several international organizations. He developed targeted universalism to promote a just society.

About Sounds True

Sounds True was founded in 1985 by Tami Simon with a clear mission: to disseminate spiritual wisdom. Since starting out as a project with one woman and her tape recorder, we have grown into a multimedia publishing company with a catalog of more than 3,000 titles by some of the leading teachers and visionaries of our time, and an ever-expanding family of beloved customers from across the world.

In more than three decades of evolution, Sounds True has maintained our focus on our overriding purpose and mission: to wake up the world. We offer books, audio programs, online learning experiences, and in-person events to support your personal growth and awakening, and to unlock our greatest human capacities to love and serve.

At SoundsTrue.com you'll find a wealth of resources to enrich your journey, including our weekly *Insights at the Edge* podcast, free downloads, and information about our nonprofit Sounds True Foundation, where we strive to remove financial barriers to the materials we publish through scholarships and donations worldwide.

To learn more, please visit SoundsTrue.com/freegifts or call us toll-free at 800.333.9185.

Together, we can wake up the world.

sounds true
WAKING UP THE WORLD